Les Parsons

Grammarama!

innovative exercises

creative activities

models from reading

sentence combining

updated rules

and more!

Pembroke Publishers Limited

© **2004 Pembroke Publishers**
538 Hood Road
Markham, Ontario, Canada L3R 3K9
www.pembrokepublishers.com

Distributed in the U.S. by Stenhouse Publishers
477 Congress Street
Portland, ME 04101-3451
www.stenhouse.com

Text Credits:
Pages 53, 65 Extracted from *Forbidden City by William Bell*. Copyright © 1990 by William Bell. Reprinted by permission of Doubleday Canada; Pages 56, 57 Reprinted from "Absolutely Invincible" by William Bell, copyright 1988. Reprinted by permission of Fitzhenry & Whiteside Limited; Page 61 Extracted from *No Signature by William Bell*. Copyright © 1995 William Bell. Reprinted by permission of Doubleday Canada; Pages 61, 62 Extracted from *Stones by William Bell*. Copyright © William Bell 2001. Reprinted by permission of Doubleday Canada.

We acknowledge the financial support of the Government of Canada through the Book Publishing Industry Development Program (BPIDP) for our publishing activities.

We acknowledge the Government of Ontario through the Ontario Media Development Corporation's Ontario Book Initiative.

Teacher Jane Graham has graciously allowed the author to adapt her concept for prepositional poetry for inclusion in this book.

National Library of Canada Cataloguing in Publication

Parsons, Les, 1943-
   Grammarama! : innovative exercises, creative activities, models from reading, sentence combining, updated rules, and more! / Les Parsons.

Includes index.
ISBN 1-55138-171-0

1. English language—Grammar—Study and teaching (Elementary)
2. English language—Grammar—Study and teaching (Secondary) I. Title.

LB1576.P364 2004   372.61   C2004-902675-5

Editor: Nancy Christoffer
Cover Design: John Zehethofer
Typesetting: Jay Tee Graphics Ltd.

Printed and bound in Canada

9 8 7 6 5 4 3 2 1

Contents

Preface   5

1. **To grammar or not to grammar?**   6
   Grammar "through the looking glass"   6
   What's your grammar?   8
   Cutting through the confusion   10
   Operator's manual   10

2. **'Do-it-yourself' grammar**   12
   A Game of "Tag"   13
   Teacher guideline: A Game of "Tag"   14
   Reading Between the Words   15
   Teacher guideline: Reading Between the Words   16
   Scrambled Adjectives   17
   Teacher guideline: Scrambled Adjectives   18
   Word Order Combinations   20
   Teacher guideline: Word Order Combinations   22
   Unsplicing Commas   24
   Teacher guideline: Unsplicing Commas   26
   Matching Parts: Correlative Conjunctions   28
   Teacher guideline: Matching Parts: Correlative Conjunctions   29
   Disjointed Sentences   31
   Teacher guideline: Disjointed Sentences   32

3. **Sentence-combining challenges**   34
   Sentence-Combining Challenge: Warm-Ups   36
   Teacher guideline: Sentence-Combining Challenge: Warm-Ups   37
   Sentence-Combining Challenge: Modifiers   39
   Teacher guideline: Sentence-Combining Challenge: Modifiers   40
   Sentence-Combining Challenge: Conjunctions   41
   Teacher guideline: Sentence-Combining Challenge: Conjunctions   43
   Sentence-Combining Challenge: Parallel Constructions   44
   Teacher guideline: Sentence-Combining Challenge: Parallel Constructions   45
   Sentence-Combining Challenge: Complex Questions   46
   Teacher guideline: Sentence-Combining Challenge: Complex Questions   47
   Sentence-Combining Challenge: Test Yourself   48
   Teacher guideline: Sentence-Combining Challenge: Test Yourself   49
   Sentence-Combining Challenge: Invent Your Own   50
   Teacher guideline: Sentence-Combining Challenge: Invent Your Own   51

4. **Learning from a pro: Reading and grammar**   52
   Clarifying the Rules   53
   Teacher guideline: Clarifying the Rules   54
   Manipulating Sentence Structure   56

Teacher guideline: Manipulating Sentence Structure *58*
Creating a Character's Language *61*
Teacher guideline: Creating a Character's Language *63*
The Power of Simple Language *65*
Teacher guideline: The Power of Simple Language *66*
Investigating Your Own Reading *68*
Teacher guideline: Investigating Your Own Reading *69*
Rubric for Investigating Your Own Reading *70*

5. Creative grammar *71*
Grammatical Nuggets *72*
Teacher guideline: Grammatical Nuggets *73*
"Tom Swifties" — Adverbial puns *75*
Teacher guideline: "Tom Swifties" — Adverbial puns *76*
Prepositional Poetry *77*
Teacher guideline: Prepositional Poetry *78*
Writing Descriptions: Less Is More *79*
Teacher guideline: Writing Descriptions: Less Is More *81*
Accidental Narratives *83*
Teacher guideline: Accidental Narratives *85*
Dueling "Diamonds" *86*
Teacher guideline: Dueling "Diamonds" *87*
Suitcase Words *88*
Teacher guideline: Suitcase Words *89*
Cooperative "Fractured" Fairy Tales *90*
Teacher guideline: Cooperative "Fractured" Fairy Tales *92*

6. Changing rules and suitable terms *93*
American English vs. British English *93*
And beginning a sentence *94*
Appropriate terminology *95*
Because beginning a sentence *96*
But beginning a sentence *97*
Can and *may* *97*
Gotten *98*
He as a gender-neutral pronoun *98*
Hopefully *99*
Indefinite pronouns in a plural sense *99*
Like *100*
Ms *101*
Prepositions ending a sentence *101*
Pronunciation *101*
Shall/will *102*
So as a conjunction *102*
Splitting infinitives *103*

Final Words: Personalizing Grammar *104*

Glossary *106*

Selected Bibliography *110*

Index *111*

Preface

The activities in this book are based on the belief that showing is better than explaining and doing is better than showing. Students will have the opportunity to explore and then build on language expertise they probably don't know they already possess. Activities and concepts will grow naturally out of concrete examples. Students will also explore the reading and writing connection by examining, reflecting on, and emulating effective models of expression.

Through a series of reproducible, ready-to-use activity sheets, students gain an in-depth understanding of how the language operates by:

- exploring, building on, and challenging their own language competencies
- identifying and correcting grammatical flaws by applying simple prompts and predictors
- examining, analyzing, and emulating models from reading
- practicing subordination and developing more complex structures through sentence combining
- applying grammar and usage concepts to creative self-expression

Grammarama was also written with the teacher in mind. Each student activity is accompanied by a comprehensive teacher guideline containing:

- background information on each concept
- specific learning objectives
- suggestions for introducing the activity
- a detailed answer key
- recommendations for group processing and bulletin board displays

Chapter 1 addresses the confusion and corrects the misinformation that commonly plagues grammar instruction. Chapter 6 presents busy teachers with an up-to-date summary of contemporary changes to traditional rules. Chapters 2 to 5 contain open-ended, reusable activities that allow students to return to and continue exploring the various concepts on a regular basis. A comprehensive glossary offers teachers capsule definitions of terms used throughout this book.

Grammarama provides numerous meaningful entry points for students who are trying to make sense of grammar, and a wealth of support and resources for the teachers who are trying to help them. If students and teachers also have some fun as they work through these activities, so much the better.

1   To grammar or not to grammar?

The never-ending controversy begins like this:

Of course you need to teach grammar! How can students learn to write properly if they don't learn how the language is constructed? How can they learn a second language if they have no formal knowledge of their first language? Besides, the brain needs the vigorous, stimulating intellectual exercise that the study of grammar offers.

Then the other camp replies:

Nonsense! Studies over the last sixty years have consistently shown that the formal teaching of grammar has had either no effect on student writing or a slight negative effect. The frustration, boredom, and confusion engendered by grammar exercises are often transferred to the task of writing itself. And apart from using a few rudimentary terms for parts of speech, how can a knowledge of grammar in one language aid a student in learning a totally different grammar in another language? Besides, everyone knows that the only way to acquire your own or a new language is not to learn about it, but to use it!

And so the theoretical battle rages.

In the day-to-day world of the classroom, however, the question of whether or not to teach grammar seldom arises. Most teachers still teach some type of formal, prescriptive grammar, and most parents would like all teachers to do so. Curriculum documents usually combine elements from both camps, and no "back to the basics" demand would be complete without a call for more grammar.

> The real question on most teachers' minds is not whether to teach grammar — but how.

The real question on most teachers' minds is not whether to teach grammar — but how.

Grammar "through the looking glass"

In Lewis Carroll's *Through the Looking Glass*, Alice and Humpty Dumpty have a discussion about words.

> *"When I use a word," Humpty Dumpty said, in a rather scornful tone, "it means just what I choose it to mean — neither more nor less."*
>
> *"The question is," said Alice, "whether you can make words mean so many different things."*
>
> *"The question is," said Humpty Dumpty, "which is to be master — that's all."*

Humpty Dumpty continues:

> *"They've a temper, some of them — particularly verbs: they're the proudest — adjectives you can do anything with, but not verbs — however, I can manage the whole lot of them!"*

We can learn a lot about the teaching of grammar by peering "through the looking glass." In Humpty Dumpty's world, words take on a character and presence that allow them to elbow their way onto the page. The medium truly is the message. In both a literal and a figurative sense, language is alive.

Grammar needs that same kind of character and presence in the classroom. If reading can enflame a passion for language, the study of grammar can just as surely dampen that passion. Far from being a written-in-stone, closed system, the language is always changing and shifting, often, for adults, in unpredictable and uncomfortable ways.

Students, on the other hand, recognize and accept this mutability. Form follows function. If they need a verbal cue signaling a quotation, they'll devise one — and adults have to come to terms with a new function for *like*. If they need a whole vocabulary to describe snowboarding, they'll invent it. If they decide that *formidable* is easier to pronounce by accenting the second syllable, they'll do so. And believe it or not, *gotten* does have a place in the English language.

These and other current usages are discussed in detail in Chapter 6. The examples are offered here to emphasize that the language is changing and that young people may be more acquainted with those changes than are adults. As teachers, we can acquaint students with their range of options, including traditional preferences, but we risk our credibility if we continually draw lines in the sand over contemporary usage. It matters what our own attitude is toward this living language. As adults, we tend to feel more comfortable with language as we were taught it when we were in school and as we used it when we were growing up. Time-honored traditions give us a sense of continuity with the past and appeal to our sense of right and wrong. But if we don't change with the changing language, we create an artificial dichotomy between language in school and language in the "real world."

Humpty Dumpty also makes it clear that language obeys the user. He perceives the struggle with language in terms of power: Who is to be the master? He sees himself as a language ringmaster managing a talented but unruly troupe, precisely the attitude we hope to nourish in students. The goal of any encounter with language in the classroom is empowerment.

The danger with grammar instruction is that students can easily feel overwhelmed and disempowered, especially with prescriptive approaches or a grammar course that seems disconnected from their everyday use of language. While they have much to learn about the complexity and sophistication of mature language users, students are not empty vessels. They are already competent in their own language milieu. Students understand communication: they need assistance in enhancing, not finding, their own voices.

Anyone who has taught students with English as their second language understands this principle. As these students explore and experiment with their new language, they often discover serendipitous and startling usages that first-language users tend to overlook. Unusual word choices or word order, odd juxtapositions, or unfamiliar phrasings can illuminate meaning in unexpected and brilliant ways. If they're taught to appreciate and retain these small triumphs, they can readily accept the myriad corrections they meet every day. They may be relatively new to English but not to language and they can teach as well as learn.

Above all, as we eavesdrop on Humpty Dumpty's lectures, we begin to appreciate that grammar needs to be playful as well as serious. And, even when

As teachers, we can acquaint students with their range of options, including traditional preferences, but we risk our credibility if we continually draw lines in the sand over contemporary usage.

it's serious, grammar doesn't have to be dull. James Joyce intrigued adults by turning language inside out; Lewis Carroll did the same thing for children of all ages. Language is actually like a multidimensional theme park with an infinite capacity to entertain and enlighten.

We need to take reading as our model. When our reading program begins to flag, we dig out a sure-fire readaloud and try to ignite a spark. If we can get students intrigued, involved, or amused, we can channel that energy and interest in all sorts of directions.

If we assume that students will learn about grammar because it's good for them, we'll run headlong into a wall of frustration. If, instead, we are constantly on the lookout for ways to intrigue, involve, and amuse our students through the study of grammar, we may just hook them on a love for language.

Delight in reading is caught not taught: so is delight in grammar.

What's your grammar?

The basic problem with teaching grammar is that the rules are often complex, arcane, and difficult to apply. The more students learn the more confused they tend to get, and the more tentative and unsure they become. There's no practical payoff for the learner. That's why a grammar program needs to be a means to an end, rather than an end in itself.

It's even difficult to be sure what people mean when they talk about grammar. Many people use the word as an umbrella term for aspects of language that aren't really grammar. Strictly speaking, a grammar is a system of rules governing the structure and arrangement of language. Usage, on the other hand, is the conventional way of dealing with particular bits of language in such areas as pronunciation, vocabulary, spelling, or syntax. Grammar — as it's taught in schools and as the public understands it — is a combination of both grammar and usage.

Even when we focus on grammar apart from usage, we still have another major problem: We don't always agree on the best way to go about teaching it. Teachers generally teach a prescriptive, descriptive, or transformational grammar or attempt a blend. Let's clarify what these approaches entail.

Prescriptive grammar

In this traditional approach, the rules that govern the use of language are taught through such practices as analyzing sentences, defining parts of speech, and distinguishing between direct and indirect objects, transitive and intransitive verbs, and active and passive voice.

The girl jumped the fence.

Girl, noun, subject of the transitive verb, *jumped*.
Fence, noun, direct object of the transitive verb, *jumped*.
The, definite article.

Descriptive grammar

This system attempts to focus on the functional relationships within language that generate the basic principles governing how the language operates. Usually, students are taught the seven basic sentence patterns in English. The three most common patterns are enough to demonstrate the method:

1. Noun phrase   Verb phrase

   People   *eat.*
   Many people   *are eating.*
   Many of the people   *are eating.*

2. Noun phrase   Verb phrase   Noun phrase

   A bee   *stung*   *the child.* (object)
   Sherlock Holmes   *was*   *a famous*
                                           detective. (complement)

3. Noun phrase   Verb phrase   Adjective

   My teacher   *is*   *very modest.* (modifier)

Transformational grammar

In this "hands-on" technique, students are required to manipulate language by expanding, rearranging, and combining sentences. Through these manipulations, students learn how to create more complex and more mature sentence patterns.

> The cap was on the table.
> The cap was blue.
> The cap was new.
> The cap was mine.
> The cap was lost.
>
> Although I thought it was lost, my new, blue cap was on the table. (combined)

As teachers, we try to simplify the language within these systems to provide students with easy-to-understand models. Unfortunately, the simple models don't always explain the complex language our students are using, or the informal usage that creates commonly used, ellipted sentences. We teach students rules and patterns to help explain their own writing, only to discover that language isn't easily pigeonholed. The models they've learned are insufficient to explain language such as:

> Between five and ten dollars seems right.
> How I do on the test depends on how hard it is.
> I don't know why he'd do something like that.
> Anything the matter?
> Here comes the teacher.

Simple models don't always explain the complex language our students are using.

The place to start is where your questions begin.
Anybody need some help?
Good to see you.
Hi.

Cutting through the confusion

The truth is that our systems of language are far more complex and riddled with inconsistencies than most of us realize. For that reason alone, students have trouble understanding what it's all about, and teachers have trouble helping them understand. By the same token, our students also know a great deal more about their own language than sometimes seems apparent to teachers.

Word order is a perfect example. How many of us realize that English imposes a strict progression when using adjectives? In sequence, we first use predeterminers (e.g., all, both, half), then determiners (articles or words that displace them), numerals, general adjectives, adjectives denoting size, age, color, and, finally, concepts, such as national origin or religious affiliation.

If we were naïve or misguided enough to prescriptively teach this word order, confusion would reign. Yet how many of our students with English as their first language would ever mix up a phrase, such as "a sweet, little, black, Persian kitten"? Given enough time and immersion in English, our students with English as a second language also learn the same word order and also without direct instruction.

Direct instruction, of course, can make a difference in how students apprehend and employ language. Students need enough grammatical terminology, for example, to allow them to talk about the various ways in which thoughts can be expressed. They need to explore how to elaborate or compress ideas in writing. They need to attend to those aspects of the language most likely to cause them to make errors considered unacceptable in standard English usage. First and foremost, however, students have to take control of and responsibility for their own learning.

In this book, students will learn by doing: The focus is on the acquisition of skills rather than the accumulation of rules. They'll be given the tools to test for errors and the options for correcting them, they'll learn how to fashion complex sentence structures and vary their usage, and they'll apply grammatical concepts to a variety of creative outlets. In the process, they should discover that working with grammar can be interesting, involving, purposeful, and just plain fun.

Operator's manual

You know your own students. You know the kinds of grammar instruction they've already encountered, their varying degrees of language facility and fluency, and their attitudes toward and interest in grammar. How many of the activities in this book you'll use, how often, and in what order will be determined by your knowledge of your students.

> In this book, students will learn by doing: The focus is on the acquisition of skills rather than the accumulation of rules.

You can easily shape and adapt the activities in this book to suit your students and the program you've developed for them. Here are a few options to consider:

- Choose one or two activities from each chapter and construct your own mini-unit.

  Chapter 2's Scrambled Adjectives
  Chapter 3's The Power of Simple Language
  Chapter 4's Modifiers
  Chapter 5's Writing Descriptions: Less is More

- Match a chapter or specific activities to complement other language texts in use.

  Chapter 4: Learning from a pro: Reading and grammar — with a literature unit or stories from an anthology
  Chapter 5: Creative grammar — as a culminating activity for a chapter in a language text
  Chapter 3: Sentence combining challenges — as a complement to your creative writing program

- Start with Chapter 5: Creative grammar as a way to engage your students' interest and demonstrate to them that grammar can be fun and useful.

- Rearrange the order in which you present the various chapters to suit your program and your students' needs.

  Chapter 4: Learning from a pro: Reading and grammar
  Chapter 3: Sentence combining challenges
  Chapter 5: Creative grammar
  Chapter 2: "Do-it-yourself" grammar

The main goal of any kind of teaching is to engage your students and keep them engaged.

The approaches to grammar offered by the various chapters in this book don't end when the activities are completed. Teachers can use a number of the activities in Chapter 2, for example, as models for constructing their own activities. Chapter 3 includes instructions for students to invent their own sentence combining exercises. In Chapter 4, a set of open-ended questions allows students to continue investigating the grammar they find in their own reading. Finally, many of the creative activities in Chapter 5 can be used whenever students are independently writing.

The main goal of any kind of teaching is to engage your students and keep them engaged. Whatever you do in the name of grammar instruction, you need to monitor your students' reactions to the program. If they're becoming resigned to, confused by, or disinterested in the program, a change is in order. *Grammarama* can help by putting you in charge of how the activities are presented and putting your students in charge of how successfully those activities unfold. Your students' grammar empowerment begins in the next chapter.

2 "Do-it-yourself" grammar

For too many students, grammar is an impenetrable fog or an endless guessing game. For others, it's a rote-learning treadmill. Whatever the perception, grammar can be a confidence shaker. Just as students begin to develop a sense of confidence and independence based on their burgeoning reading and writing competencies, their struggles with grammar undermine that confidence and leave them dependent on the teacher. The teacher assumes the mantle of grammar expert: The teacher has all the answers.

But what would happen if students began to question that basic assumption? What if they came to realize that they already possessed a certain amount of language expertise themselves? How would their attitudes toward and success with grammar change if they could independently access, examine, and learn from their own language competencies? What would it do for their confidence if they could apply simple prompts and predictors on their own to identify and correct grammatical flaws?

The activities in this chapter are based on the assumptions that students already know a lot about language that they can put to good use and that they can independently figure out a lot more. In some of the activities they're offered challenges to solve through their own competencies; in others, they're given basic tools and techniques and encouraged to apply them.

A great deal of collaboration and sharing is built into the activities. Students often work in small groups to allow them to pool their resources, compare their results, and learn from one another. A variety of solutions to the challenges are often possible: Students learn that language is flexible and multi-leveled rather than a rigid sequence of right and wrong answers. In some cases, students are offered a creative or expressive follow-up to extend the learning and reinforce the concept that grammar is a means to an end rather than an end in itself. Chapter 5: Creative grammar is devoted to this essential principle.

The dynamics of these lessons allow teachers to take on a different role. Instead of stepping into the spotlight as the "sage on the stage," teachers are able to function as the "guide at the side." Although teachers will introduce and manage these grammar activities, students will perceive that, for the most part, they can definitely do it themselves.

Instead of stepping into the spotlight as the "sage on the stage," teachers are able to function as the "guide at the side."

A Game of "Tag"

Part A

Turn the following statements into questions by adding the appropriate "tag."

1. That girl is clever, _____ ?
2. You couldn't have told twelve people my secret, _____ ?
3. I'm not going to lose again, _____ ?
4. The stars of the show usually sign autographs, _____ ?
5. You will give that back, _____ ?
6. Everybody likes pizza, _____ ?
7. You used to own a dog, _____ ?
8. We're allowed to walk on the grass, _____ ?
9. You paid for the tickets, _____ ?
10. Please accept this with my compliments, _____ ?

Part B

In groups of three or four, compare your answers to the questions in Part A. Place a check mark beside the tags on which you all agree. If you disagree about a tag, choose the one from your group that sounds the most natural, or discuss the question later on with the larger class group.

Part C

People who learn English as a second language usually have a lot of difficulty with these kinds of tag questions. Why do you think this construction is difficult to learn? What advice, if any, can you offer about how to construct these kinds of questions?

Part D

Follow the format of Part A to create five tag questions of your own. Use a blank line for the actual tag. Exchange with a partner and complete each other's questions. Check your partner's answers. If disagreements about appropriate tags arise, discuss them later on with the large class group.

A Game of "Tag"

Background

In French, you can change a statement into a question simply by adding the tag, "n'est-ce pas?" This translates roughly into "isn't that so?"

Elle est tres intelligent, *n'est-ce pas?*
You've got your lunch money, *n'est-ce pas?*

We do the same thing in English, but, unlike the second example above, it's far more complicated. Instead of tagging one phrase equivalent to *n'est-ce pas* at the end of statements, we use many different phrases. All sorts of rules govern this complicated usage, but we don't seem to need them. Students with English as a first language possess an intuitive sense of the correct usage. Students who learn English as a second language, however, have enormous difficulties phrasing these kinds of questions.

Any explanation of the mechanics of this usage would be so complicated and confusing that it would be useless as a guide. The best way to learn them is to experience them over and over as we listen and read.

Learning objectives

• To review and build on students' understanding of tag questions.
• To share expertise about tag questions in small groups.
• To generate practical advice for constructing these kinds of questions.

Activity introduction

Write the following statement on the board:

That player is terrific.

Remove the period and add a comma and a lined space ending with a question mark.

That player is terrific, _____ ?

Ask the students how to complete the blank in order to turn the former statement into a question.

When the example is finished, explain that this type of construction is called a "tag." Make the connection with the French usage, *n'est-ce pas* and discuss how the English construction differs. Discuss and assign the student activity.

Answer key

Part A

1. isn't she? 2. could you? 3. am I? 4. don't they? 5. won't you? 6. don't they? 7. didn't you? 8. aren't we? 9. didn't you? 10. won't you?

Part B

Ask the groups to report on which tags seemed to be the most confusing and how disagreements were resolved.

Part C

As the small groups report back to the large class group, post and discuss the kinds of advice generated in their discussions.

Part D

Ask which tags seemed problematic and discuss why that might be.

Reading Between the Words

Part A

The expression, "reading between the lines" refers to an added meaning suggested but not explicitly stated in something we read. In this exercise, you need to do even more than that. For each of the sentences below, fill in one word for each space to create a correct, meaningful statement. You may use each word only once. Be creative: Any number of variations are possible.

1. a. We saw _____ _____ _____ car.

   b. He bought _____ _____ _____ shirt.

   c. She built _____ _____ _____ house.

2. a. She looked _____ _____ _____ table.

   b. We swam _____ _____ _____ lake.

   c. He ran _____ _____ _____ park.

3. a. He _____ _____ over _____ _____ .

   b. She _____ _____ on _____ _____ .

   c. We _____ _____ beyond _____ _____ .

4. a. _____ _____ can't _____ _____ now.

   b. _____ _____ won't _____ _____ early.

   c. _____ _____ should _____ _____ safely.

Part B

The opening stanza of Lewis Carroll's poem "Jabberwocky" from *Through the Looking Glass* sounds at once strange and familiar. Most of the words are nonsense, but they're arranged in patterns we recognize. After your teacher reads the poem aloud, "read between the words" and draw a picture on the back of this page of what you imagine the scene to be. Label as much of your drawing as you can with words from the poem.

Jabberwocky

'Twas brillig, and the slithy toves
Did gyre and gimble in the wabe:
All mimsy were the borogroves,
And the mome raths outgrabe.

Reading Between the Words

Background

Syntax is the pattern or structure of word order in sentences. We are so attuned to syntax and to making sense out of what we read that we tend to fill in missing parts when we're presented with sentence fragments. That tendency is known as grammatical closure.

Cloze passages rely on this tendency and are often used to increase students' awareness of and sensitivity to the grammar of written language. They also help students make appropriate substitutions as they focus on the meaning of text.

You can easily create your own cloze passages by adapting a paragraph or two from a fiction or nonfiction text. If you want to focus on nouns, for example, simply blank them out in the passage and ask students to fill in the blanks with words that make sense in context.

Be prepared for variations when students fill in the blanks. If you're working with an adapted passage, accept any answer that makes sense.

Learning objectives

- To increase students' awareness of syntax through cloze passages.
- To reinforce students' understanding of selected parts of speech.
- To increase students' awareness of and sensitivity to syntax by creating their own context.

Activity introduction

Part A

Write the following sentence on the chalkboard:

If you know the _____ to the _____ , raise your _____ .

Ask the students to fill in the blanks. Then ask them how they knew what to put in each blank. From a discussion of making sense out of text and our understanding of syntax, direct them to complete Part A of the student activity.

Part B

After you read the poem aloud (*gyre*, by the way, is pronounced with a soft "g" and *gimble* with a hard "g"), you might mention that *'Twas* is an abbreviated form of *It was*. Reassure the students that drawing ability has no bearing on this exercise and that there is no one correct interpretation.

Answer key

Part A

When you take up the exercise, accept any answer that makes sense. After you finish with a section, discuss the kinds of words that the structure forced them to use, e.g., adjectives in question #1, prepositions in #2, verbs and nouns in #3, and nouns or pronouns in #4.

Part B

The syntax will direct students to accept certain words as nouns, verbs, and adjectives. Some students will be embarrassed by their drawing skills or the fact that the poem hasn't stimulated their imaginations. Accept whatever they come up with. You might ask them to put a check mark in the corner of the page if they agree to make their drawing public. A bulletin board display of these drawings will allow you to draw attention to the similarities and differences.

Scrambled Adjectives

When we string adjectives together to describe a noun, we usually don't think about their order. If English is our first language, we simply put them in the order that seems right. In spite of the fact that a number of rules govern the arrangement of adjectives, we learn to put them in order by ourselves and, in most cases, correctly.

In the following exercise, five nouns are preceded by blank spaces for adjectives that describe them. The adjectives for each noun are scrambled and listed by number. Complete Part A individually and without discussion. Then move on to Part B.

Part A

Put the adjectives assigned to each noun in the order that seems most usual and natural and write them in your final order in the spaces provided.

1. _____ _____ _____ _____ _____ kitten
2. _____ _____ _____ _____ _____ retrievers
3. _____ _____ _____ _____ _____ speeches
4. _____ _____ _____ _____ _____
_____ students
5. _____ _____ _____ _____ _____ _____
_____ sports cars

1. black a Persian little sweet
2. brown two Labrador old big
3. presidential these endless campaign all
4. determined Quebec both English those young
5. Italian half red these great big eight

Part B

In groups of three or four, compare your results. Whenever results differ, discuss the justification for each one and select the version that sounds most usual and natural. For a different perspective, you might start with each adjective alone with the noun and add the others in one by one. Sometimes, however, a slightly different word order offers a slightly different meaning; in that case, both versions would be acceptable. For example, "my new best friend" and "my best, new friend" mean two different things and both would be correct.

Part C

When your group has agreed as best as you can on the correct versions for each noun phrase, carefully examine the results. What rules governing word order for adjectives can you figure out from the five examples? Write down your rules.

Scrambled Adjectives

Background   Contrary to popular belief, word order matters in English. Adjectives, for example, are placed in sequence in front of nouns in a specific order:

1. predeterminers — such as *all*, *both*, *half*
2. determiners — articles or words that displace them, such as *a*, *the*, *these*, *her*
3. numerals — ordinal and cardinal, such as *third* or *three*
4. general adjectives — such as *extraordinary*
5. size
6. age
7. color
8. concepts — such as national origin, religious affiliation

As we listen and read, the correct order quickly becomes intuitive. Students with English as their first language seldom mix up this order unless they are presented with an unusually large number of adjectives. The sequence for using adjectives is never formally taught. Students with English as a second language, however, often have considerable difficulty with this kind of word order until immersion in the language internalizes the sequencing. Much the same kind of difficulty arises when English speakers begin to learn French and are presented with the problem of whether a particular adjective precedes or follows a noun.

Learning objectives
- To acquaint students with the concept that English has strict rules governing word order.
- To give students hands-on practice in placing adjectives in the correct order.
- To enable students to deduce some of the rules governing word order with adjectives.

Activity introduction   Write the following sentence on the chalkboard: *She wore blue beautiful old necklace to school.* Ask the students to identify what's wrong with the sentence and how they would go about correcting it. Discuss how they know to put adjectives in a certain order. Then ask them to differentiate between the following two phrases:

1. My last funny story
2. My funny last story

In the first example, a number of other stories could have been written since the author wrote a funny story. They just didn't happen to be funny stories. In the second example, it's clear that the last story the author wrote was a funny one.

Answer key   The answers in Parts A & B are listed on the following page. Sample variations are given in brackets.

1. a sweet little black Persian kitten (little sweet)
2. two big old brown Labrador retrievers (brown old)
3. all these endless presidential campaign speeches
4. both these determined young Quebec English students
5. half these eight great big red Italian sports cars

In Part C, students will probably offer descriptions for some of the categories. They might say *how much of something* for predeterminers or *what you think about it* for general adjectives. You can supply the standard label as the need arises or if you wish. This additional information is for their interest alone. No attempt should be made to memorize or test the categories or their order. The categories are listed on page 18.

Word Order Combinations

The meaning of a sentence changes depending on how the words are arranged. In the following example, the same four words are rearranged in six different combinations to produce six different meanings. Notice how the punctuation changes to agree with the new arrangement and new meaning.

1. Susan won't change it.
2. Won't Susan change it?
3. It won't change, Susan.
4. It won't change Susan.
5. Won't it change, Susan?
6. Won't it change Susan?

Use this pattern as your model and create five more sentences for questions 1-3. In questions 4 and 5, the pattern changes. Use only the words from the original sentence and use all of them each time. You will need to change the punctuation.

1. *_____ can't help it.
   (* Place your own name in the blank.)
   a. _____
   b. _____
   c. _____
   d. _____
   e. _____

2. Teachers won't fail students.
   a. _____
   b. _____
   c. _____
   d. _____
   e. _____

3. The students don't want any pets.
   a. _____
   b. _____
   c. _____
   d. _____
   e. _____

Word Order Combinations — *continued*

4. It is not too hard to see most animals.

    a. _____

    b. _____

    c. _____

    d. _____

    e. _____

5. All the cars could not have broken down at once.

    a. _____

    b. _____

    c. _____

    d. _____

    e. _____

Word Order Combinations

Background
A myth endures that word order in English is not that important. As the Scrambled Adjectives activity in this chapter demonstrates, the opposite is true. In the Word Order Combinations activity, the importance of word order is illustrated with every word in a sentence. An entire sentence is rearranged to produce six different sentences with six different meanings. Although punctuation is altered or added to reinforce the meaning, all the words are used each time and no words are added.

As they manipulate the assigned sentences and experiment with various combinations, students will come to appreciate the importance of word order and the flexibility of the language. They will also realize that they have sufficient fluency and facility to manipulate the language purposefully and independently.

Learning objectives
• To demonstrate the importance of word order in English.
• To develop a feeling of language competency.

Activity introduction
Place the example sentences from the student activity sheet on the chalkboard. Read the sentences aloud with intonation to emphasize their differences. Discuss the changes in punctuation and how these changes affect the meaning.

When you assign the exercise, remind students to use the example sentences as a model for the first three sets of sentences and develop their own sentences following the same pattern. Remind them that the pattern changes for the final two sets of sentences. Their challenge is to use all the words in any five different combinations.

Answer key
1. NAME can't help it.
   a. Can't NAME help it?
   b. It can't help, NAME.
   c. It can't help NAME.
   d. Can't it help, NAME?
   e. Can't it help NAME?

2. Teachers won't fail students.
   a. Won't teachers fail students?
   b. Students won't fail teachers.
   c. Students won't fail, teachers.
   d. Won't students fail, teachers?
   e. Won't students fail teachers?

3. The students don't like any pets.
   a. Don't the students like any pets?
   b. The pets don't like any, students.
   c. The pets don't like any students.
   d. Don't the pets like any, students?
   e. Don't the pets like any students?

4. It is not too hard to see most animals.
   a. Is it not too hard to see most animals?
   b. It is too hard to not see most animals.
   c. Is it too hard to not see most animals?
   d. Is it not hard to see most animals, too?
   e. Is it hard to not see most animals, too?

5. All the cars could not have broken down at once.
   a. Not all the cars could have broken down at once.
   b. Could all the cars not have broken down at once?
   c. Could not all the cars have broken down at once?
   d. The cars could not all have broken down at once.
   e. Not all at once could the cars have broken down.

Unsplicing Commas

When two independent sentences are joined only with a comma, the error is called a *comma splice*.

> My homework was almost finished, there was one question left.
> I was relieved when I got my test back, I didn't make one mistake.

Identifying the splice

There is a simple test to detect a comma splice. Check the structure on either side of the comma. If they both can be turned into questions that can be answered "yes" or "no," then they are indeed independent sentences and you have detected a comma splice.

> Was my homework almost finished? **Yes.**
> Was there one question left? **Yes.**

> Was I relieved when I got my test back? **Yes.**
> Didn't I make one mistake? **No.**

If a question based on a structure can't be answered "yes" or "no," then it's not a comma splice and the comma is correctly used.

> When I got home, it was almost dark.
> I got home when? **Not applicable.** (This structure can't be answered "yes" or "no.")
> Was it almost dark? **Yes.**

If no verb is present in the structure, it's not a comma splice. Since you can't turn the structure into a "yes" or "no" question, the test still works even if you're uncertain whether or not a verb is present.

> Renata, my best friend, gave me a present.

Renata by itself can't be turned into a question. *My best friend* by itself can't be turned into a question. *Gave me a present* by itself can't be turned into a question.

Correcting the splice

Comma slices can be corrected by replacing the comma with a period, a semicolon, or the coordinate conjunction, *and*.

> I was relieved when I got my test back. I made only one mistake.
> I was relieved when I got my test back; I made only one mistake.
> I was relieved when I got my test back and I made only one mistake.

Unsplicing Commas — *continued*

In the following passages, apply the comma splice test every time a comma is used. If no verb is present in the structure write "NA" (for Not Applicable) over top of the comma. When you encounter two structures you're not sure of, write the questions with the appropriate "yes" or "no" or "NA" for the answers. When you identify a comma splice, correct the error using whichever of the three options you feel is most appropriate.

1. The cafeteria was crowded. I looked around for a seat, nothing was available. When I checked again, I saw a seat beside a friend of mine.
2. Alicia, Ahmed, and James raced down the stairs. They had to run, they were late for class.
3. Andrea, my best friend, gave me a present. I opened it up, there was a book inside.
4. Roger was born in London, Ontario. As the years went by, his parents moved to Vancouver, Toronto, and then back to London. Roger felt that London was home, he was glad to be back.

Unsplicing Commas

Background

The comma splice is defined with examples of the error in the student activity sheet. Once they're focused on the error, of course, students tend to find it everywhere a comma is used. Try to help them narrow that focus. The two structures first have to be sentences; they must contain a verb. If a comma separates two or more nouns or modifiers and no verbs are present, then it can't be a comma splice.

The two structures also have to be independent sentences; subordinate clauses are by definition dependent. Alert them to spotting subordinate conjunctions, such as *unless, when, while, since, as,* or *although.* Subordinate conjunctions make one idea dependent on another and are used when it makes more sense to show a cause and effect relationship or emphasize the order in which things happen.

Keep in mind, as well, that students may encounter the incorrect practice in their reading, since some contemporary writers tend to view the usage as a viable, stylistic option.

The student activity sheet also shows students how to identify and correct the splice.

> *Comma slices can be corrected by replacing the comma with a period, a semi-colon, or the coordinate conjunction,* and.
> *I was relieved when I got my test back. I made only one mistake.*
> *I was relieved when I got my test back; I made only one mistake.*
> *I was relieved when I got my test back and I made only one mistake.*

If your students are unfamiliar with semicolon usage, introduce it now. Explain that these punctuation marks are sometimes used to join two independent but related statements; they also separate items in a series that already contain punctuation.

> I like basketball; however, I never watch it on television.
> The goals were scored by Alicia Day, Gr. 7, Ms Cooper's class; Keisha Henry, Gr. 8, Mr. Liu's class; and Opal Chan, Gr. 8, Ms Reid's class.

As soon as you introduce the semicolon, of course, expect to see it spring up like weeds in your students' writing. Teaching the uses of the semicolon is much easier than teaching moderation in the use of the semicolon.

Learning objectives

- To identify comma splices by means of a test.
- To correct comma splices in one of three ways.

Activity introduction

Introduce the error through the explanations and examples from the student activity sheet.

Answer key

1. "Did I look around for a seat?" **Yes**
   "Was nothing available?" **No**
   A correction: "I looked around for a seat. Nothing was available."
   "When I checked again," **NA (subordinate clause)**
   or
   "I checked again when?" **NA (can't be answered "yes" or "no")**

2. "Alicia, Ahmed, and James" **NA (no verb)**
   "Did they have to run?" **Yes**
   "Were they were late for class?" **Yes**
   A correction: "They had to run; they were late for class."

3. "Andrea," **NA (no verb)**
   "my best friend" **NA (no verb)**
   "Did I open it up?" **Yes**
   "Was there a book inside?" **Yes**
   A correction: I opened it up and there was a book inside.

4. "London, Ontario" **NA (no verb)**
   "As the years went by" **NA (subordinate clause)**
   or
   "The years went by as?" **NA (can't be answered "yes" or "no")**
   "Vancouver, Toronto" **NA (no verb)**
   "Did Roger feel that London was home?" **Yes**
   "Was he glad to be back? **Yes**
   A correction: "Roger felt that London was home; he was glad to be back."

Matching Parts: Correlative Conjunctions

When using conjunctions in pairs, you're supposed to balance them off with the same kind of sentence parts. *Either . . . or* is one set of correlative conjunctions. Notice in these examples how the sentence parts after the conjunctions match:

> I think I'll have either *a hamburger* or *a salad.* (balancing nouns)
> I'll either *do my homework tonight* or *finish it tomorrow.* (balancing verb phrases)
> I left my keys either *in the change room* or *on the bus.* (matching prepositional phrases)

By making the parts match, you keep the order straight in the reader's mind and allow the rhythm to make the meaning more memorable.

Other common correlative conjunctions are:

neither . . . nor	both . . . and
although . . . nevertheless	although . . . yet
if . . . then	just as . . . so
not only . . . but also	since . . . therefore
When . . . then	whether . . . or

Your challenge is to choose five of the above pairs of correlative conjunctions. Write two sentences using each set. Be sure the sentence parts match after each conjunction in the set.

Matching Parts: Correlative Conjunctions

Background

This activity focuses on parallelism when employing correlative conjunctions. The student activity sheet lists a number of common correlative conjunctions and explains why parallelism or "matching parts" is an effective, stylistic technique.

You can extend this concept by discussing parallelism with lists. Items in a list should be expressed using the same part of speech, for example, all nouns or all adjectives. The reader's innate appreciation of order and balance is disrupted by mixtures. Here are some examples of faulty parallel structures and possible corrections:

Faulty: The student was diligent, personable, and an athlete.
Corrected: The student was diligent, personable, and athletic.

Faulty: He ran smoothly, quickly, and without a lot of effort.
Corrected: He ran smoothly, quickly, and effortlessly.

Faulty: She liked to play basketball, to watch movies, and hanging out at the mall.
Corrected: She liked to play basketball, to watch movies, and to hang out at the mall.

Learning objectives

- To introduce the concept of parallelism when using correlative conjunctions.
- To practise using parallelism when using correlative conjunctions.

Activity introduction

Put on the chalkboard the examples of faulty parallelism in lists from the teacher background section. Direct students to examine the list in the first sentence and identify the part of speech of each item in the list. Discuss the concept of parallelism and ask how that list might be improved. Do the same with the other examples.

Caution the students that sometimes a list may not look balanced because part of the sentence is understood but not written.

I don't know whether to have fries with my hamburger or (to have) a salad.

Move on to the student activity introduction and the concept of parallelism using correlative conjunctions.

Answer key

Answers will vary. A sample sentence for each set of correlative conjunctions follows:

Neither . . . nor
Neither my mother *nor* my father could come to the concert.

Both . . . and
I have trouble *both* with writing compositions *and* with editing them.

Although . . . nevertheless

Although I've never played in a band, *nevertheless* I'll give it a try.

Although . . . yet
Although they raised a lot of money for charity, *yet* they felt disappointed about not raising more.

If . . . then
If we can't go to the movies Thursday night, *then* we'll go Friday night.

Just as . . . so
Just as you would like to be treated, *so* you should treat others.

Not only . . . but also
We *not only* have to study for a history test *but* we *also* have to prepare for an English quiz.

Since . . . therefore
Since you didn't bring in your permission form, *therefore* you can't go on the excursion.

When . . . then
When I don't hear from her for a couple of days, *then* I get worried.

Whether . . . or
I don't know *whether* to choose the red shirt *or* to choose the blue shirt.

Disjointed Sentences

Sometimes when we're writing, the main part of a sentence and the modifying part don't make sense together. What we want to say and what we write turn out to be two different things.

In our heads, for example, we think: "After borrowing a pen, I quickly finished the homework." What we write is: "After borrowing a pen, the homework was quickly finished." If you look closely at the second sentence, you'll notice that *the homework* has borrowed a pen. The two parts of the sentence have lost their true connection and now don't make sense.

This problem frequently arises when we leave participles "dangling." A participle is either the "ing" form of a verb (such as *falling*) or the past form, such as those ending in "ed" (such as *talked*) or "en" (such as *forbidden*). Participles are frequently used as adjectives. Participles in a phrase are often used to modify the subject of the sentence.

Flipping through her math book, she turned to the day's assignment.

Flipping is the participle, *flipping through her math book* is the phrase, and the participial phrase modifies the subject *she*. We say the participle is "dangling" if it doesn't have anything to modify that makes sense.

Flipping through her math book, the day's assignment was found.

In this case, it seems as if the assignment was flipping through the book. Since that doesn't make sense, the participle is "dangling."

Examine the list of twelve sentences for "dangling" participles. When you identify the modifying phrase, ask yourself who is involved in the action. If the answer doesn't make sense, then the participle is "dangling." Some of the sentences make sense as they are. If there's nothing wrong with the sentence and it makes sense the way it is, leave it that way. If the sentence does not make sense, you need to fix it.

1. Watching from high in the stands, the football player seemed very tiny.
2. Running as fast as possible, the bus still left without me.
3. Swooping over the trees, the seagull finally landed on the beach.
4. When trying to steer on an icy road, your car can go out of control.
5. After writing for half an hour, I was only half finished the exam.
6. Worried about her grades, more studying seemed like a good idea.
7. After finishing their homework, Mother gave the children an extra hour of television.
8. Thinking about the math test, she realized it wouldn't be hard to get a passing grade.
9. Opening her locker, a book fell out.
10. Sleeping until noon, her Saturday was ruined.
11. Tired of standing in a lineup, the movie no longer seemed like such a good idea.
12. Forbidden to exercise until his broken leg healed properly, gym classes were out of the question.

Disjointed Sentences

Background

Reading and writing are rooted in the search for meaning. We read and write to make sense of and to cope with the world. Although participles and "dangling" participles are defined in the student activity sheet, they aren't the true focus of this activity.

Instead of trying to memorize a definition for participles or to identify them in sentences, students should be examining sentences to see if they make sense. If they can see where and how meaning becomes disjointed, they can correct the flaw. Whether or not they can remember the technical name for the error is a minor consideration.

The ultimate goal is to send them back to their own writing empowered to independently revise for meaning.

Learning objectives

- To practise identifying disjointed sentences.
- To practise rephrasing sentences with "dangling" participles.

Activity introduction

If students find a sentence with a "dangling" participle, they either rephrase the main part of the sentence to give the participle something to modify, or rephrase the participle to include the subject. Their challenge is to make the sentence make sense.

Place the following sentence on the chalkboard:

> After trying out for the soccer team, the volleyball team was her second choice.

Through discussion, elicit these possible corrections:

Correction 1: After trying out for the soccer team, she made the volleyball team her second choice.

Correction 2: After she tried out for the soccer team, she made the volleyball team her second choice.

Correction 3: After she tried out for the soccer team, the volleyball team was her second choice.

When assigning the twelve sentences, emphasize the search for meaning, remind students that some sentences are perfectly fine as written, and stress that there are several ways to correct the sentences containing errors.

Answer key

Some students will try to rephrase the principal clause and some will rephrase the participle. Since your goal is to have students identify disjointed sentences and then correct them, all corrected sentences should be accepted.

Two corrected versions are supplied for each of the assigned sentences. More are possible.

1. Watching from high in the stands, we noticed that the football player seemed very tiny.
   As we watched from high in the stands, the football player seemed very tiny.

2. Running as fast as possible, I still watched the bus leave without me.
   Although I ran as fast as possible, the bus still left without me.

3. No error.

4. When trying to steer on an icy road, you can find your car going out of control.
   When you steer on an icy road, your car can go out of control.

5. No error.

6. Worried about her grades, she decided that more studying was a good idea.
   Since she was worried about her grades, more studying seemed like a good idea.

7. After finishing their homework, the children got an extra hour of television from their mother.
   After the children finished their homework, their mother gave them an extra hour of television.

8. No error.

9. Opening her locker, she noticed a book fall out.
   When she opened her locker, a book fell out.

10. Sleeping until noon, she ruined her Saturday.
    Since she slept until noon, her Saturday was ruined.

11. Tired of standing in a lineup, we no longer thought the movie was such a good idea.
    When we got tired of standing in a lineup, the movie no longer seemed like such a good idea.

12. Forbidden to exercise until his broken leg healed properly, he knew gym classes were out of the question.
    Since he was forbidden to exercise until his broken leg healed properly, gym classes were out of the question.

3 Sentence-combining challenges

Sentence combining is a relatively straightforward teaching technique in which students build a single, complex sentence from a series of simple sentences. Combining sentences leads students to link and subordinate ideas and develop a more varied, fluid, and mature writing style. Sentence combining can be viewed as the flip side of the study of models. Rather than examining and analyzing exemplary writing samples, students build their own exemplary samples from some simple raw materials.

A simple sentence is often defined as a single statement of fact in the form of a subject (what you're talking about) and a predicate (what you want to say about it).

I have a dog. His name is Spot. Spot likes to run. Spot likes to play.

The sentences above are grammatically correct, but hardly effective. Grammatically correct and grammatically effective are two different concepts. Overusing simple sentences creates and encourages monotony, a lack of thematic emphasis, and a disconcertingly choppy, disjointed rhythm.

Deciding whether or not a sentence is effectively structured, unfortunately, can be tricky. Students who attempt to remedy this flaw may find a grammatically correct solution to be even less acceptable.

I have a dog and his name is Spot and Spot likes to run and Spot likes to play.

Since all the statements are strung together like beads on a necklace, they're all equally weighted. It's difficult to sort out the importance of one idea from another in the monotonous, linear repetition. On the other hand, be careful of imposing hard and fast rules. Joining a series of simple statements with *and* is usually considered a weak and inadequate option. Nevertheless, students will find numerous examples of professional writers effectively using that very construction.

There's no one right answer to a sentence-combining exercise. A teacher who favors the construction, "My dog, Spot, likes to run and play." still has to credit the student who comes up with "I have a dog named Spot who likes to run and play." As long as the final sentence is correctly and effectively structured, it's acceptable.

Sentence-combining exercises can be completed in a class group, in smaller groups, or as an individual, independent activity. The technique is ideally suited, however, for problem solving in small groups. Teachers who use the technique this way should ask a scribe from each group to write the group's final sentence combinations on chart paper or on an overhead projector

There's no one right answer to a sentence-combining exercise. As long as the final sentence is correctly and effectively structured, it's acceptable.

transparency. The various solutions from each group can then be examined and discussed in a large-group context.

Although it's a proven and valuable tool for improving student writing, sentence combining has to be implemented carefully. Here are some practices to emulate and some to avoid:

- Do play up the problem solving nature of the exercises. Try to make it fun.
- Don't overuse the technique. The goal is always to turn students back to their own writing. A little practice out of the context of the writing process goes a long way.
- Do vary how the exercises are completed. If you use some of the exercises for individual, independent seatwork, make sure you precede that strategy with lots of small-group, problem solving discussions.
- Don't limit the number of solutions. Accept anything that works. While some solutions may be more effective or flow more naturally than others, often it's a matter of personal preference. Encourage students to discover as many ways as possible to acceptably combine the sentences and use that variety as a springboard to discuss the relative merits of each.

Encourage students to discover as many ways as possible to acceptably combine the sentences and use that variety as a springboard to discuss the relative merits of each.

Sentence-Combining Challenge: Warm-Ups

Although short, simple sentences can be used effectively, too many of them can make your writing seem repetitive, choppy, and not connected well. The challenge in the following questions is to create one correct and effective sentence out of each series of short, basic sentences.

> Sample
>
> It was dark.
> It was stormy.
> It was night.
> I was lost.
>
> I was lost on a dark and stormy night. (combined)

The sentences in most of the following questions can be combined in more than one way. Find the construction that you feel is the most naturally flowing and effective.

1. Her backpack was bulging.
   Her backpack was heavy.
   Her backpack was full.
   It contained overdue library books.

2. The mall was crowded
   The young people were excited.
   The record store was holding a sale.
   The sale was 50% off all CD's.

3. The teacher looked for his eyeglasses.
   He looked for them in his coat pockets.
   He looked for them on his desk.
   He looked for them in the staff room.
   He found them on his nose.

4. She looked at the history assignment.
   It was long.
   It was complicated.
   It was due next week.
   She made a decision.
   She decided not to start it right away.

5. He looked at his English notebook.
   It was the night before the exam.
   The exam was important.
   Pages in his notebook were missing.
   Pages in his notebook were illegible.
   Pages in his notebook were incomplete.
   His heart sank.

Sentence-Combining Challenge: Warm-Ups

Background   This activity serves as an initial introduction to sentence combining. As you work through the example in the student activity sheet, include the following process fundamentals and routines that will support all subsequent sentence-combining challenges:

Fundamentals

1. The goal of sentence combining is to help students develop a more mature, versatile, and complex writing style. The focus should be on applying what they learn from the exercises to their own writing.
2. Most of the exercises can be answered in a variety of ways. Choosing from among various correct options will help them identify and develop their own personal preferences.
3. Correct solutions are not always effective solutions. Students should strive for correct, fluid, natural-sounding phrasings.

Routines

1. Students most often work on solutions in small groups.
2. Each group collects as many correct solutions as they can come up with.
3. They evaluate the solutions for the one or two they feel are the most effective.
4. Someone from the group writes their final solutions on chart paper or over-head transparency to share with the rest of the class.

Learning objectives
- To introduce students to the strategy of sentence combining.
- To introduce students to the process fundamentals and routines that will be used throughout this chapter.
- To afford students practice in sentence combining and in evaluating their solutions.

Activity introduction

1. Place this example on the chalkboard:

   Ian studied.
   Ian studied all night.
   He studied for a geography exam.
   He arrived at school.
   He was dismayed.
   He found out he had studied for the wrong exam.

2. Explain that all the sentences in the example are grammatically correct. Ask what's wrong with writing this way?
3. Explain that sentence combining activities will help them recognize when and how to change repetitive, choppy, and disjointed sentences in their own writing to more mature, complex, and effective sentences.
4. Explain that in these activities, their challenge is to combine a series of short, simple sentences into one correct and effective sentence. Place the example from page 38 on the chalkboard. Explain that this solution sentence is grammatically correct, and ask what's wrong with it.

Ian studied all night and it was for a geography exam and he arrived at school and he was dismayed because he had studied for the wrong exam.

Challenge students to offer more effective solutions to the example. Possible solutions might be:

- Although Ian had studied all night for a geography exam, he was dismayed when he arrived at school to find out he had studied for the wrong exam.
- After studying all night for a geography exam, Ian was dismayed to find out when he arrived at school that he had studied for the wrong exam.
- Since (even though) Ian studied all night for a geography exam, when he arrived at school he was dismayed to find out he had studied for the wrong exam.

Answer key   One solution is supplied for each question in the student activity. Students will probably develop other, equally valid solutions that should be accepted.

1. Her heavy, bulging backpack was full of overdue library books.
2. When the record store held a 50% off all CD's sale, excited young people crowded the mall.
3. As Jason looked at his English notebook the night before the important exam, his heart sank when he saw missing, illegible, and incomplete pages.
4. After the teacher looked for his eyeglasses in his coat pockets, on his desk, and in the staff room, he found them on his nose.
5. When Sophie examined the long, complicated history assignment due next week, she decided not to start it right away.

Sentence-Combining Challenge: Modifiers

Adjectives and adverbs — called modifiers — add specific, concrete detail to your writing. Where and how you place modifiers, however, can enhance or change a sentence's meaning. The challenge in the following questions is to skilfully position the modifiers as you create one correct and effective sentence out of each series of short, basic sentences.

Sample

> The principal always read the announcements.
> He read them every morning.
> He read them slowly.
> He read them haltingly.
> He read them in a monotone.
> No one listened.
>
> Since the principal always read the morning announcements in a slow, halting monotone, no one listened. (combined)

The sentences in most of the following questions can be combined in more than one way. Find the construction that you feel is the most naturally flowing and effective.

1. The monkey bars were in the park.
   They were painted blue.
   They were painted yellow.
   They were painted red.
   They were newly painted.
   High school students were playing on them.

2. The pizza looked delicious.
   It contained double cheese.
   It contained pepperoni.
   It contained anchovies.
   It was stone cold.

3. There were two dogs.
   They were big.
   They were brown.
   They were Labs.
   They were straining on their leashes.
   They were trying to chase cars.
   They were tied to a fire hydrant.

4. Tanya started her homework.
   She started it reluctantly.
   The homework was math.
   She broke her pencil.
   She broke it unexpectedly.
   She couldn't continue.

5. Rahid rummaged through the bottom of his locker.
   He was looking for his history text.
   He found two library books.
   They were overdue.
   He found three gym socks.
   They were grass-stained.
   He found a rotting apple.
   It was half-eaten.
   He found four lunches.
   They were uneaten.
   He found his planner.
   It was long lost.

Sentence-Combining Challenge: Modifiers

Background This activity explores the best ways to inject adjectives and adverbs into descriptions. Students may not be aware, however, that where and how modifiers are placed can enhance or change a sentence's meaning. The suggested introduction to the activity highlights this issue. Since students already have experience completing sentence-combining exercises, you can narrow the focus of your introduction.

Learning objective • To practice sentence combining with an emphasis on modifiers.

Activity introduction 1. Place the following sentences on the chalkboard:

The car was blue.
The car had a yellow racing stripe on the side.
It was new.

2. Ask students to combine the sentences in two different ways with two different meanings.

The new blue car had a yellow racing stripe on the side.
The blue car had a new yellow racing stripe on the side.

3. Mention that several questions in the activity will present them with a similar choice.

Answer key One or two solutions are supplied for each question in the student activity. Students will probably develop other, equally valid solutions that should be accepted.

1. High school students were playing in the park on the newly painted, red, blue, and yellow striped monkey bars.
2. Although the double cheese, pepperoni, and anchovy pizza looked delicious, it was cold.
    or
    The cold, double cheese, pepperoni, and anchovy pizza looked delicious.
3. Two, big, brown Labs, tied to a fire hydrant, were straining on their leashes trying to chase cars.
4. When Tanya reluctantly started her math homework, she unexpectedly broke her pencil and couldn't continue.
5. As Rahid rummaged through the bottom of his locker looking for his history text, he found two, overdue library books, three grass-stained socks, a rotting, half-eaten apple, four uneaten lunches, and his long-lost planner.

Sentence-Combining Challenge: Conjunctions

Conjunctions allow you to link up ideas in your writing. *Coordinate conjunctions*, such as *or*, *and*, or *but*, connect words, phrases, or sentences that are equal in value and make sense joined together.

Sample

You're my friend.
I'm not going to loan you money.

You're my friend, but I'm not going to loan you money.
(combined)

Subordinate conjunctions, such as *unless*, *when*, *while*, *since*, or *although*, are used when it makes more sense to show a cause and effect relationship or emphasize the order in which things happen. Subordinate conjunctions make one idea dependent on another.

Sample

Raymond went to the washroom.
Someone took his eraser.

When Raymond went to the washroom, someone took his eraser. (combined)

The challenge in the following questions is to use conjunctions as you create one correct and effective sentence out of each series of short, basic sentences. Most of the following questions can be combined in more than one way. Find the construction that you feel is the most naturally flowing and effective.

1. The assembly was in the auditorium.
   The students were noisy.
   The principal walked onto the stage.
   The students got noisier.

2. The rollerbladers came down the pathway.
   There were two of them.
   They were middle-aged.
   They were zigzagging.
   They were out of control.
   They didn't know how to stop.

3. It was lunchtime.
   Bob ate a French fry.
   He ate another one.
   He ate another one.
   His friend noticed.
   His friend yelled, "Get your dirty fingers out
     of my French fries!"

4. Ashante had left studying until the last
     minute.
   English was her favorite subject.
   She was confident.
   She thought she would still do well.

5. We had looked forward to seeing the new
     movie.
   We wanted to see it as soon as it opened in
     the theatres.
   We took one look at the lineup for tickets.
   It went around the block.
   We decided to go home.

Sentence-Combining Challenge: Conjunctions

Background

Coordinate and subordinate conjunctions are abstract concepts that are difficult for students to absorb. Students need to encounter numerous concrete examples before they understand how conjunctions operate.

Through sentence combining, students first recognize how conjunctions function and then actively employ them. Since they are learning through doing, they are more apt to transfer the concepts to their own writing.

Learning objectives

- To recognize the functions of coordinate and subordinate conjunctions.
- To practise using conjunctions to clarify and facilitate meaning.

Activity introduction

The introduction from the student activity sheet should be enough to get the students started. Before they start, however, be sure to stress that there are more conjunctions than are listed in the introduction and that they are free to use any that suit their purposes as they combine sentences. In this regard, when taking up the solutions, you might list the conjunctions students used that weren't mentioned in the introduction.

Common coordinate conjunctions are:

And, but, for, nor, or, so, yet

Common subordinate conjunctions are:

After, although, as, as if, as long as, because, before, even though, if, provided, while, like, since, so that, unless, until, when, whenever, where, wherever, why

The relative pronouns *who*, *which*, and *that* and the interrogative pronouns *who*, *which*, *what* also serve as subordinating conjunctions.

Answer key

One solution is supplied for each question in the student activity. Students will probably develop other, equally valid solutions that should be accepted.

1. When the principal walked onto the auditorium stage, the noisy students in the assembly only got noisier.
2. Since they didn't know how to stop, the two, middle-aged rollerbladers came zigzagging out of control down the pathway.
3. After Bob ate two French fries one after another at lunchtime, his friend noticed and yelled, "Get your dirty fingers out of my French fries!"
4. Although Ashante had left studying until the last minute, English was her favorite subject and she was confident she would still do well.
5. Even though we had looked forward to seeing the new movie as soon as it opened in the theatres, we took one look at the lineup for tickets going around the block and decided to go home.

Sentence-Combining Challenge: Parallel Constructions

Expressing several ideas in a series in the same grammatical construction helps to show how those ideas are linked and makes the phrases flow in a natural and balanced fashion. In the examples that follow, the parallel constructions are marked in italic.

Sample

She went *around* the corner, *down* the stairs, and *into* the office.

The student was extremely *intelligent*, naturally *witty*, and generally *hard-working*.

Trying to reach class before the bell, he *raced* down the hall, *jumped* over a garbage can, and *staggered* into the classroom.

The challenge in the following questions is to use parallel constructions to create one correct and effective sentence out of each series of short, basic sentences. The sentences in most of the following questions can be combined in more than one way. Find the construction that you feel is the most naturally flowing and effective. Underline the parallel constructions in your final sentences.

1. The puppy was black and white.
   The puppy was cute.
   The puppy raced down the hall.
   The puppy stumbled.
   The puppy tumbled head over heels.
   The puppy landed in a pile of dirty clothes.

2. The teacher couldn't find the daybook.
   The teacher didn't understand the assignment.
   The teacher wasn't expecting the first class.
   The teacher was a substitute.

3. The lock on Natalie's locker wouldn't open.
   She shook it.
   She pulled on it.
   She hit it with a book.
   She noticed it wasn't her locker.

4. The students were in the band.
   They were seniors.
   They were very experienced.
   They were unusually talented.
   They were well prepared.

5. We were in gym class.
   We were training outside for cross-country.
   We struggled up hills.
   We scrambled down hills.
   We leaped over ditches.
   We dashed across fields.
   We felt like a pack of hounds chasing a fox.

Sentence-Combining Challenge: Parallel Constructions

Background

All students use prepositions, modifiers, and verbs in their writing. They often spontaneously use two of the same type in a series. Using three or more, however, requires a thorough understanding of parallel construction and a conscious intent to link and balance similar phrasings for effect.

When students encounter parallel constructions in their reading, they're probably unaware of how or why the writing has been deliberately fashioned. Since the phrasing is so smooth-flowing and sounds so natural, the reader stays caught up in the meaning.

Sentence combining demonstrates to students the value of parallelism and affords them opportunities to practise the technique.

Learning objectives

• To increase students' awareness and understanding of parallel constructions.
• To give students opportunities to devise parallel constructions.

Activity introduction

The introduction to the student activity illustrates three examples of parallel construction. Remind students that they should underline the parallel constructions in their final solution sentences.

Answer key

One solution is supplied for each question in the student activity. Students will probably develop other, equally valid solutions that should be accepted.

1. The cute, black and white puppy <u>raced</u> down the hall, <u>stumbled</u>, <u>tumbled</u> head over heels, and <u>landed</u> in a pile of dirty clothes.
2. The substitute teacher <u>couldn't find</u> the daybook, <u>didn't understand</u> the assignment, and <u>wasn't expecting</u> the first class.
3. When the lock on Natalie's locker wouldn't open, she <u>shook</u> it, <u>pulled</u> on it, and <u>hit</u> it with a book until she noticed it wasn't her locker.
4. The senior students in the concert band were very <u>experienced</u>, unusually <u>talented</u>, and well <u>prepared</u>.
5. Training outside in gym class for cross-country, we <u>struggled up</u> hills, <u>scrambled down</u> hills, <u>leaped over</u> ditches, and <u>dashed across</u> fields like a pack of hounds chasing a fox.

Sentence-Combining Challenge: Complex Questions

We normally think in terms of simple questions:

> When's lunch?
> Is this for homework?
> Who's finished?

We sometimes construct more complex questions when we're trying to qualify the answer or use the question as part of an argument.

> If you didn't want me to tell the truth, why did you ask me the question?

In this exercise, several statements are followed by a simple question. Your challenge is to combine those statements and the question into one, complex question.

Sample

You have lots of time to study.
You have a good set of notes to study from.
You have a quiet, comfortable place to study.
Why aren't you studying?

Since you have lots of time, a good set of notes, and a quiet, comfortable place to study, why aren't you studying? (combined complex question)

---

1. You're going to play baseball after school.
   You're going to a movie after dinner.
   When were you planning to do your homework?

2. I have lettuce for a salad.
   I have mushrooms for a salad.
   I have green onions for a salad.
   I have red pepper for a salad.
   What else do I need to make a salad?

3. Chelsea tried unsuccessfully to borrow money
      from her mother.
   Chelsea tried unsuccessfully to borrow money
      from her father.
   Chelsea tried unsuccessfully to borrow money
      from her brother.
   Who should she try next?

4. Ali didn't study for his last English test.
   Ali spent very little time on his book report.
   Ali didn't hand in his last writing assignment.
   Why does Ali still expect to do well in English?

5. I looked for my sweater in the hallway.
   I looked for my sweater in my last class.
   I looked for my sweater in my locker.
   Where else should I look for my sweater?

6. Lots of people have a pen like that.
   The pen has no distinguishing marks.
   Dani says the pen is hers.
   How can you be sure the pen is yours?

Sentence-Combining Challenge: Complex Questions

Background

Most students normally think in terms of simple questions: How are you? Where are you going? What are you doing after school? They seldom construct complex questions containing qualifying subordinate clauses.

> Even if you've never borrowed money from me before and you've promised to pay me back, why should I loan you ten dollars?

These kinds of questions arise when people are reasoning through a logical sequence or trying to develop a cause and effect relationship in their arguments. The qualifications tend to limit the kind of response possible or even to make the question hypothetical.

This activity encourages students to explore the structure of these kinds of complex sentences and demonstrates how they can expand their own style of questioning in their speaking and writing.

Learning objective

- To practise developing a complex question from a series of simple statements and a simple question.

Activity introduction

The student activity sheet introduces the concept and method in detail. Review the instructions orally to ensure that students understand the assignment. You may also want to collaboratively combine the sentences in question #1 with the class as a whole to make sure that students are clear about the process before they begin working independently.

Answer key

One solution is supplied for each question in the student activity. Students will probably develop other equally valid solutions that should be accepted.

1. If you're going to play baseball after school and then go to a movie after dinner, when were you planning to do your homework?
2. Since I have lettuce, mushrooms, green onions, and red pepper, what else do I need to make a salad?
3. After Chelsea tried unsuccessfully to borrow money from her mother, father, and brother, who should she try next?
4. Since Ali didn't study for his last English test, spent very little time on his book report, and didn't hand in his last writing assignment, why does he still expect to do well in English?
5. Now that I've looked for my sweater in the hallway, in my last class, and in my locker, where else should I look?
6. Since lots of people have a pen like that, it has no distinguishing features, and Dani says it's hers, how can you be sure the pen is yours?

Sentence-Combining Challenge: Test Yourself

The following questions offer you the opportunity to gauge how well you can manipulate modifiers and use conjunctions and parallel constructions as you try to create one correct and effective sentence out of each series of short, basic sentences.

Remember that most of the following questions can be combined in more than one way. Find the construction that you feel is the most naturally flowing and effective.

1. The bell rang to change classes.
   The students streamed into the halls.
   They were talking.
   They were laughing.
   The teachers watched them.
   The teachers were amused.

2. The skateboarder was small.
   The skateboarder was wide-eyed.
   The skateboarder shot down the sidewalk.
   The skateboarder dodged a group of school kids.
   The school kids were shrieking.
   The skateboarder jumped over a bench.
   The bench was at the bus shelter.
   The skateboarder ran into a police officer.
   The police officer was tall.
   The police officer was outraged.

3. The student performers were talented.
   They put on a musical.
   The musical was thrilling.
   It was colorful.
   It was fun-filled.
   It was based on the *Wizard of Oz*.

4. The morning bell had rung.
   It had rung five minutes ago.
   Students lined up at the office.
   The students numbered in the dozens.
   They were quiet.
   They were patient.
   They were polite.
   They were waiting for their late slips.

5. Santos was explaining.
   Santos was explaining in vain.
   Santos was explaining to his teacher.
   The teacher taught him English.
   Santos didn't have his homework.
   Santos' dog had eaten his homework.
   The English teacher was sceptical.

Sentence-Combining Challenge: Test Yourself

Background These exercises review the sentence-combining techniques covered to this point and prepare students for the creative application to follow.

  If you would like to continue with sentence combining in a more extended and comprehensive fashion, the following resource may be helpful:

  Strong, William. *Sentence Combining: A Composing Book*. 3rd ed. New York: McGraw-Hill, 1994.

Learning objective • To review and practise sentence-combining concepts and techniques.

Activity introduction Remind the students that the exercises will require them to combine modifiers, use conjunctions, and employ parallel constructions. As always, most of the challenges can be combined in a variety of ways.

Answer key One solution is supplied for each question in the student activity. Students will probably develop other, equally valid solutions that should be accepted.

1. When the bell rang to change classes, the amused teachers watched the talking, laughing students stream into the halls.
2. The small, wide-eyed skateboarder shot down the sidewalk, dodged a shrieking group of school kids, jumped over a bench at the bus shelter, and ran right into a tall, outraged police officer.
3. The talented student performers put on a thrilling, colorful, fun-filled musical based on *The Wizard of Oz*.
4. Since the morning bell had rung five minutes ago, dozens of quiet, patient, polite students lined up at the office waiting for their late slips.
5. Santo was explaining in vain to his sceptical English teacher that he had done his homework but his dog had eaten it.

Sentence-Combining Challenge: Invent Your Own

Your challenge is to create your own sentence-combining puzzles by inventing five series of short, simple sentences for someone else to solve. Here's how to proceed:

1. Choose a theme or situation, such as a sport, a pet, learning to rollerblade, or going to a movie.
2. Visualize a scene based on your choice: What's going on? Who's involved?
3. Describe that scene in one of two ways:
   a. Write one complex sentence and then break it up into a series of short, simple sentences.

   > After Alex dove smoothly into the pool, swam quickly to the surface, and pulled himself effortlessly out of the water, he tripped on a towel and fell right back in.

   Series: Alex dove into the pool.
   He dove smoothly
   He swam to the surface.
   He swam quickly.
   He pulled himself out of the water.
   He pulled himself effortlessly.
   He tripped on a towel.
   He fell right back in the water.

   With this approach to the task, you know ahead of time that the series of short sentences you eventually wind up with will combine effectively. The main challenge to this approach is creating that original sentence.

   b. Begin with one short sentence, add another related sentence, and continue building the sentences one by one as you get a sense of how the idea is growing and where it's going to lead. Then test it out to see if the series can be effectively combined into one complex sentence. If not, you will have to make some adjustments.

   Series: The guitarist played with enthusiasm.
   The guitarist played with passion.
   The guitarist played with great skill.
   His electric guitar was unplugged.
   No one could hear him.

   > Although the guitarist played with enthusiasm, passion, and great skill, since his electric guitar was unplugged, no one could hear him.

   The strength of this approach is that you only need one short, simple sentence to begin. The main challenge is that you're never really sure if the series can be combined until you do it yourself.

   With either approach, you end up creating both the series of short, simple sentences and at least one combined solution.

4. When you're finished your five series of sentences, exchange them with a partner and solve each other's sentence-combining puzzles. Compare and discuss each other's solutions.

Sentence-Combining Challenge: Invent Your Own

Background This activity serves as an intermediary step for students between completing sentence-combining exercises and applying the concepts and techniques to their own writing. This creative, hands-on challenge gives them the opportunity to internalize what they've learned. The approach also affords them flexibility in how they visualize and complete the activity. Students have the option of working from simple to complex or from complex to simple.

Learning objective • To review and practise sentence-combining concepts and techniques.

Activity introduction The student activity sheet provides step-by-step instructions in how to proceed. Review them orally to ensure that students understand the assignment.

Answer key The activity includes a process for self-correction. Students exchange their sentences with a peer and then compare and discuss their solutions. If they disagree about the validity of a particular solution, they can then turn to the teacher for guidance. You may also want to extend the activity in one of several ways:

• Ask students to submit one of their favorite groups of core sentences and compile them in a sentence-combining exercise for the whole class, possibly on chart paper or on an overhead transparency.
• In small groups, students exchange their core sentences, combine them, and compare solutions.
• Students examine their reading material for sentences they can deconstruct into simple sentences or combine into more complex sentences. Ask them to submit five examples, citing the source for each.
• Students examine a recent sample of their own writing for sentences they can deconstruct into simple sentences or combine into more complex sentences. Ask them to submit five examples, citing the source for each.

4 Learning from a pro: Reading and grammar

Students can learn a great deal about style from professional writers, including the rules of grammar they follow and the rules they consciously modify.

We spend a lot of time in schools asking students what they understand from their reading; we spend relatively little time asking them what they think about how that reading is constructed. The most-used reading activities, for instance, involve students in recalling, copying, and demonstrating facts; in other words, proving that they've read what they were supposed to read. The least-used reading activities call upon students to summarize or synthesize material or analyze an author's style. Students can learn a great deal about style from professional writers, including the rules of grammar they follow and the rules they consciously modify. This chapter helps students become aware of and appreciate the techniques that professionals use to achieve their desired effects.

Whether we're reading what someone else has written or writing ourselves, the manner in which language is manipulated affects how successfully the message will be received. Writers manipulate language to achieve specific effects. Grammar, usage, and spelling are part of the language palette from which effective writers choose when crafting their stories. As we start to analyze why we respond the way we do to effective writing, we become more aware of that craft. When we can appreciate the finished product as well as the plan that produced it, our emotional understanding is fused with an intellectual understanding. The combination is far more powerful than its separate parts.

The study of models is a proven technique for helping students understand the grammar of the language and, in the process, improve their writing. Since the activities that follow are based on excerpts from the writing of only one author, William Bell, the stylistic diversity is obviously purposeful. The selected models offer a window into a few of the numerous techniques at the disposal of a professional writer and the diverse effects created by deliberate choice.

William Bell has a wealth of technical expertise at his disposal. This award-winning Canadian author has also been a high school English department head in Ontario and an instructor at universities in Harbin and Beijing, China, and at the University of British Columbia.

In each of his best-selling novels, Bell weaves one or more social issues within a compelling, character-driven, and realistic narrative. The stories examine these issues from a variety of perspectives as characters struggle with difficult choices and unsettling conflicts. Thus, students learn more about their world and, in the process, examine their own emerging beliefs and values.

The following bibliography of Bell's young-adult fiction is ordered chronologically, beginning with his most recent novel (* indicates novels from which excerpts have been taken for this chapter):

- Alma
- Stones*
- Zack
- Speak to the Earth
- No Signature*
- Forbidden City*
- Five Days of the Ghost
- Absolutely Invincible*
- Crabbe
- Death Wind

Clarifying the Rules

Teachers are fond of saying that you have to learn the rules of writing before you can break them. It might be more accurate to say that you need to learn what the rules are before you can follow them. In this excerpt from one of William Bell's novels, no "rules" are broken even though it may seem that way at first.

In *Forbidden City*, seventeen-year-old Alex Jackson comes home from school to find that his father, a news camera operator, wants to take him to China's capital, Beijing. The following passage occurs soon after Alex arrives in Beijing. He and his father are invited to a formal Chinese banquet. As you read this description, consider why so many of the sentences have no verb.

> *The waiters and waitresses started bringing in the hot courses. Each time a dish arrived the top would be removed with a flourish and the waiter would announce the name of it — in Chinese. We got deep-fried chicken, and chicken balls in oyster sauce. Two or three kinds of fish served on big oval platters — fish with the heads and tails still on and the eyes staring at you, daring you to eat. Slices of duck with crisp, fatty skin. Shrimps with hot red sauce that made my eyes water. Shredded pork with green pepper and black mushrooms. Beef bits with ginger and onions.*

1. a. The last five sentences have no verb. Bell could have listed the same information in several different ways. Brainstorm with a partner to determine some other ways. Rewrite the verbless sentences using one of those other choices.

   b. What kind of information is being presented in this description? Compare your version with Bell's. Why do you think he chose to present the information in sentences without verbs?

2. *"We got deep-fried chicken, and chicken balls in oyster sauce."*
   A comma doesn't seem to be required in this sentence. Why do you think Bell used one? Why is "deep-fried" hyphenated?

3. a. Bell uses a dash twice in this paragraph. How would you explain this use of the dash?

   b. If Bell hadn't used a dash, how else might he have written these sentences? Why do you think he chose to use the dash?

Clarifying the rules

Background   Student writers often harbor misconceptions about how language operates. They firmly believe that all sentences must have a subject and a verb, for example, when grammarians have identified ten types of verbless sentences. They also have an incomplete sense of when to use a comma and tend to avoid using a dash at all costs. These flawed "rules" frequently become ends in themselves.

As they examine this excerpt from William Bell's *Forbidden City*, students will begin to appreciate that clarity of expression is the primary goal of a knowledgeable and skilful writer and that form always follows function. Once they understand what the rules actually are, student writers can concentrate on how best to get meaning across to a reader.

As you discuss what a sentence may or may not be, this definition may prove useful.

A sentence contains a word or words grouped together to convey meaning, often, but not always, containing two elements: what you are talking about (the subject) and what you want to say about it (the predicate).

Learning objectives   • To explore clarity of expression through the use of a model.
• To clarify the use of a verbless sentence, a dash, a hyphenated phrasal adjective, and a comma separating two coordinated clauses.

Activity introduction   Since this activity is the first in the chapter, you may want to use the biographical information from the chapter introduction to familiarize students with William Bell's background and achievements. They may also be interested in learning that his books have been translated into nine languages.

The student activity sheet introduces the actual assignment. The answer key explains the rules that Bell followed in the model.

Answer key   The detailed answers in this key are supplied only as a shorthand guide to the content. They shouldn't be viewed as a standard against which student answers are judged. Depending on their age and stage of reading fluency, students will express these ideas in their own language and according to their own background and experiences.

1. a. The narrator is relating a list of food dishes. Since the context is understood and the verb is implicit, Bell presents each dish on the page as it was presented in real life. Each dish is spotlighted and highlighted in its own sentence.

   The verbless sentence is a special technique designed to produce a specific effect. It should be used carefully and sparingly. If the idea in a verbless sentence is communicated completely and effectively, however, the usage is legitimate.

   b. Bell could have listed the dishes using a colon and commas or commas alone.

   We got the following dishes: deep-fried chicken, and chicken balls in oyster sauce, two or three kinds of fish served on big oval platters — fish with the heads and tails still on and the eyes staring at you, daring you to eat, slices of duck with crisp, fatty skin, shrimps with hot red sauce that made my eyes water, shredded pork with green pepper and black mushrooms, and beef bits with ginger and onions.

With either of these methods, you lose the sense of ceremony in the actual presentation style and any appreciation of the uniqueness of each dish is lost in a jumble of details.

2. Normally a comma wouldn't be used to separate two coordinated clauses. In this case, however, the comma is used to avoid ambiguity. Without the comma, the reader might assume that both the deep-fried chicken and the chicken balls were in oyster sauce. The comma makes it clear that only the chicken balls were in sauce.

"Deep-fried" is an example of a phrasal adjective: two words joined together to form a phrase modifying a noun that follows them. You wouldn't use a hyphen if you wrote "The shrimp were deep fried."

3. a. The dash provides a break in a sentence for several reasons: to separate a parenthetical remark, to replace a colon, or to add emphasis in a series of statements separated by commas. The dash (—) is represented in keyboarding as two hyphens. In books, the dash would not have a space between.

   b. In the first sentence, Bell could have left out the hyphen — and lost the emphasis. In the second sentence, he could have used a comma. In this case, the qualifying phrases pile up one on top of another and clarity is lost.

Manipulating Sentence Structure

Part A

In the opening to the novel *Absolutely Invincible*, we meet George Ma, a fifteen-year-old refugee from an unnamed South Asian country. Although he's highly intelligent, fluent in English, and quite skilled in a form of unarmed self-defence, called Shaolin, he is crippled by a loss of short- and long-term memory, the result of a horrific incident in his past. Notice how the author deliberately manipulates George's use of grammar and the effects the author creates in the process.

> *I remember some things.*
>
> *Bob and Mitzi, who take care of me. Where I live. Shifu and my workouts at the gym. I can read now, and do some arithmetic.*
>
> *And at night sometimes, the strange dream with the jungle and the storm and the voice that screams over broken teeth.*
>
> *But inside my head shadows fall on empty spaces. Things that happen, words people say, faces, thoughts — all get lost. They disappear.*
>
> *I am in a washroom at the school.*
>
> *There is a big, half-circle sink with a mirror above it. I stare at the face in the mirror. Dark hair, dark eyes. The face is blank. Nothing to see there. Only shadows.*

1. a. Underline the sentences that lack a subject and/or a predicate.
   b. As the story unfolds, we discover that George speaks fluent English. What is the author trying to suggest about George by having him think in these kinds of sentence fragments?

2. *"**And** at night sometimes, the strange dream with the jungle **and** the storm **and** the voice that screams over broken teeth."*
   Try saying this sentence aloud a few times to get a feeling for the rhythm and the mood. What is the mood and how is it created? Why do you think the author used three *and's* in this sentence?

3. *"I stare at the face in the mirror. Dark hair, dark eyes. The face is blank. Nothing to see there. Only shadows.*
   The author uses a combination of short declarative sentences and sentence fragments as George stares at his reflection in the mirror. Say them aloud. What impression do you get of the mind behind the face in the mirror? What creates this impression?

4. Notice the use of paragraphing in this passage. Three of the paragraphs are single sentences. The rest are brief collections of short sentences or sentence fragments. Why does the author paragraph this way?

Manipulating Sentence Structure — *continued*

Part B

Now compare that first excerpt with a passage from much later in the novel. George and a small group of friends strengthen and support each other. As his trust in these friends has grown, and through their encouragement and patient attention, George has been transformed. His short-term memory is now normal and fragments of his past are returning. His confidence in his own abilities has grown dramatically. He and his friends are about to begin a motorcycle trip and he's taking his first solo ride through the countryside in the early morning.

> *The white lines flash away behind me. The road blurs past, rushing under my feet. I lean into the curves, steering with my weight. I crank the right handgrip and the speedometer needle jumps to sixty-five and the engine grumbles a little louder.*
>
> *Above and ahead of me I see a hawk floating up in the clear sky. He is like a sharp pencil point, writing invisible circles on the blue as he rides the wind. Below him, I am gliding inches above the blacktop, drawing an invisible line on the earth. There are no cars ahead and nothing in my mirrors.*

1. What changes from the passage in Part A do you notice in the kind of sentences used and the way the paragraphs are formed? What do these changes suggest about George and his condition?
2. In the second paragraph above, to what does George compare himself? From the images used here, how would you describe his state of mind and what leads you to this understanding?

Manipulating Sentence Structure

Background

This activity explores how grammar can be shaped to suggest a character's state of mind using excerpts from William Bell's *Absolutely Invincible*. The narrator of the story is George Ma, a fifteen-year-old refugee from an unnamed South Asian country. Students shouldn't attribute the fragmented nature of George's thoughts in the first of the two excerpts either to the problems of a second-language learner or to a lack of intelligence. George is fluent in English as the second of the two excerpts clearly illustrates.

The characteristics of George's initial thoughts have been carefully crafted to reflect his emotional state of mind. A childhood trauma is buried in the depths of George's shattered memory. The first excerpt gains its power partly from the unusual and unexpected structure of the sentences and paragraphs fashioned to resonate with the results of that trauma.

Since your discussions will revolve around how sentences and paragraphs are supposed to be constructed, the following definitions may prove useful:

A *sentence* is comprised of a word or words grouped together to convey meaning, often, but not always, containing two elements: what you are talking about (the subject) and what you want to say about it (the predicate).

A *paragraph* contains one or more sentences about a single topic, grouped together, and usually with an indented first line.

Learning objectives

• To review how sentences and paragraphs are constructed.
• To demonstrate how the structure of sentences and paragraphs can be manipulated for effect.

Activity introduction

Write the following fragments on the chalkboard:

"Hello."
"Don't!"

Ask students if they consider these fragments to be sentences. If not, why not? If so, how would they define the term sentence?

Expect a variety of answers and comments. Some students will repeat definitions they've learned over the years. Others may talk about subjects and predicates or express the concept of making sense or getting an idea across or even having a part of a sentence understood but not explicitly stated. At this stage, you want them reflecting on what they think they know, and possibly acknowledging that the definition of a sentence is not as clear cut as they might believe.

At some point in the discussion, you can move directly into the student activity sheet for a writer's perspective on what a sentence should or should not be.

Answer key

The detailed answers in this key are supplied only as a shorthand guide to the content. They shouldn't be viewed as a standard against which student answers are judged. Depending on their age and stage of reading fluency, students will express these ideas in their own language and according to their own background and experiences.

Part A

1. a. The underlined sentences lack a subject and/or a predicate.

    > I remember some things.
    >   <u>Bob and Mitzi, who take care of me.</u> <u>Where I live.</u> <u>Shifu and my workouts</u>
    > <u>at the gym.</u> I can read now, and do some arithmetic.
    >   <u>And at night sometimes, the strange dream with the jungle and the storm</u>
    > <u>and the voice that screams over broken teeth.</u>
    >   But inside my head shadows fall on empty spaces. Things that happen,
    > words people say, faces, thoughts — all get lost. They disappear.

    > I am in a washroom at the school.
    >   There is a big, half-circle sink with a mirror above it. I stare at the face in
    > the mirror. <u>Dark hair, dark eyes.</u> The face is blank. <u>Nothing to see there.</u> <u>Only</u>
    > <u>shadows.</u>

    b. The sentence fragments reflect the fragmented nature of George's
        thoughts. Students may remark on the simple, stilted language or the
        disordered, piecemeal aspects of his thought processes. They may also
        pick up on the fact that he remembers few details of the world around
        him and few people. His sparse, random thoughts are expressed in simple,
        concrete terms.

2. This fragment has a nightmarish quality induced by the linking of the
    words *night, strange, jungle, storm, screams,* and *broken teeth.* We don't
    know what it all means but it sounds terrifying, especially the idea of
    screaming over broken teeth. The first *and* links this sentence with the
    things he remembers and also propels us directly into the dream with no
    warning or introduction, in the same way that dreams or nightmares
    often begin. The other *and's* tie all the strange images together and force
    us to attend to them and make sense out of them together.

3. George stares at his face as though it's the face of a stranger. His inner
    mind is closed and empty of thought and memory. Taken together, the
    words *dark, blank, nothing,* and *shadows* paint an impressionistic picture
    of his mind's murky, impenetrable void.

4. The short paragraphs serve several functions. They reflect the fact that
    George thinks in brief, sporadic bursts dealing with one simple subject at a
    time. They also draw attention to and emphasize the content.

    I remember some things underscores that George is about to tell us
    something of importance about himself. The punctuation at the end of
    the sentence could have been a colon instead of a period, but George isn't
    capable at this time of creating formal lists.

    The next paragraph is so brief and disconnected that we immediately
    understand that something is seriously wrong. The dream fragment is
    shockingly and dramatically set off in a paragraph by itself for maximum
    impact. The final paragraph of this section highlights the fleeting nature of
    all these thoughts.

Part B

1. The sentences all have subjects and predicates. They are longer and more purposeful, flowing, and complex. The paragraphs are longer and the content is rich in detail and fluidly and coherently organized.

   George is now completely aware of and in touch with his environment. He is confident in his ability to master complicated tasks and seems totally integrated with his surroundings. The growth in his expressive language reflects the growth in his emotional state of mind.

2. George clearly identifies with the hawk — strong, free, and facing limitless horizons. George seems disentangled from his past and positive about the future.

   The hawk *floats* and George *glides.* The hawk writes *invisible circles* on the sky; George draws *an invisible line* on the earth. As he looks in his mirrors, George sees no danger behind him and, as he looks through the windshield, no danger ahead.

Creating a Character's Language

If you want to create believable, three-dimensional characters, you have to pay attention to the language they use. The physical details you invent as you describe a middle-aged lawyer are wasted if the character talks like a teenage skateboarder. The way characters express themselves should be consistent with who they are.

Part A

One of the themes in William Bell's novel, *No Signature*, is adult illiteracy. A boy and his father have been estranged for ten years; the reason hinges on the father being unable to read and write and trying to keep the fact secret from everyone. In the following passage, the father explains how he's been able to cope in the world without being able to read and write.

> *"If you can't read, you've gotta get by with word of mouth, you've gotta ask directions all the time. People naturally tell me street names, thinkin' I'll find the signs, so I ask them about landmarks — you know, a gas station or a big, gray building, whatever. I can read numbers, as long as they're not too long, so I can follow a map because all the highways are numbered. If I'm goin' somewhere, I count the towns I'll pass through on the way. Then when I think I'm where I want to be, I stop at a gas station or a restaurant and shoot the breeze for a few minutes and then say, 'What town is this, anyway? I missed the sign.'"*

1. Focus on how this character talks rather than on what he's trying to communicate. What clues suggest that he lacks a formal education?
2. To be articulate means to be able to express yourself clearly and fully. How articulate is this character, and on what do you base your opinion?
3. What's the difference between intelligence and literacy? What evidence can you find that demonstrates this character's intelligence?

Part B

Bell changes the structure of a character's language for an entirely different reason in his novel, *Stones*. Although *Stones* is set in the present day, a diary from 1827 is pivotal to the plot. The diary was written by a young English woman who had settled in the wilderness of what is now Ontario, Canada to start a farm. You may be unfamiliar with some of the vocabulary. *Homespun* refers to cloth woven at home; homespun clothing would be simply made and plain-looking. *Stout* means strong or solidly made.

> *Yesterday morning, as I was working in the kitchen garden, there emerged from the trees on the edge of the west field a figure whose uncommon appearance startled me more than I care to admit, for her structure was tall and straight and her skin coal black. She wore homespun, with a bandana of white on her head and stout, if rather the worse for wear, boots on her bare feet.*

Creating A Character's Language — *continued*

She greeted me politely, her words conveyed with a lilt and flow not at all familiar to my ears, and said that she and her husband Jubal Duvalier had located on the third line to the west of us.

Her name was Hannah, she said, and she was looking for work, and, as I had now two babies to care for . . . .

1. Underline any phrases or word order that seem odd or old-fashioned to you. Why did Bell write the diary this way if the language or manner of expression makes it more difficult to read?
2. What guesses can you make about the narrator's background or character from the nature and content of her writing?
3. An ellipsis (. . .) is used at the end of sentences to indicate that the sentence is unfinished. How would you fill in the missing part of the last sentence?
4. Rewrite the first paragraph in one of two ways:
   - in language you would use if you were writing in your own diary today;
   - as a six-year-old child of the past or today.

   Use as many sentences as you need. Change vocabulary, word order, and punctuation in any way you like.

Creating a Character's Language

Background

Students are often unaware of the craft that goes into creating a believable character. As they read professionally written material, they're drawn into a character's life without noticing the conscious technique that influences their perceptions.

Many student writers pour most of their own efforts into moving along the plotline and describing concrete, physical details. Not surprisingly, most of their characters talk the way they and their friends talk.

In this activity, students explore how and why an author purposefully manipulates the language a character uses. They also have an opportunity to practice those same skills themselves.

You might want to incorporate the Writing Descriptions: Less Is More activity from Chapter 5: Creative grammar as a logical follow-up at the end this activity.

Learning objectives

- To increase awareness of how and why an author manipulates a character's language.
- To practice creating language consistent with a character's identity.

Activity introduction

Direct students to listen to a brief monologue and make whatever assumptions they can about that character based on the way the character talks. Then read aloud the following excerpt:

> *"So we were gonna see a movie last night an' he was like what do you wanna see an' I was like I dunno an' then he was like really what do you wanna see an' I was like I really dunno. An' I could see he was gettin' a little ticked off an' I woulda said but like I really didn' know and then he was like are you gonna say and I was like why do I hafta say?"*

After discussing their observations, move on to the introduction to the student activity sheet.

Answer key

The detailed answers in this key are supplied only as a shorthand guide to the content. They shouldn't be viewed as a standard against which student answers are judged. Depending on their age and stage of reading fluency, students will express these ideas in their own language and according to their own background and experiences.

Part A

1. Students will mention some of the following clues:
   - uses *gotta* for *got to*
   - drops "g's" on *thinking* and *going*
   - employs relatively simple vocabulary; a preponderance of one-syllable words
   - uses colloquial expressions, such as *shoot the breeze*
   - utilizes little subordination, principal clauses linked with commas or *so*

2. The father is highly articulate. In short order, he's able to state in general why his condition makes it so difficult to cope in the world and then offers a series of specific examples to illustrate how he's been able to overcome his disability.

3. In a world that assumes that everyone knows how to read, the father has been able to devise strategies that allow him to travel wherever he wants to go and, at the same time, to hide his disability. He has been able to maintain his independence, his personal freedom, and his self-esteem by living by his wits.

Part B

1. Depending on the age and background of the students, they may choose any number of details that seem odd or old-fashioned. Some of the more obvious are underlined below:

> *Yesterday morning, as I was working in <u>the kitchen garden</u>, <u>there emerged from the trees</u> on the edge of the west field <u>a figure</u> whose <u>uncommon appearance</u> startled me more than I care to admit, for <u>her structure was tall and straight</u> and her skin coal black. She wore <u>homespun</u>, with a bandana <u>of white</u> on her head and <u>stout</u>, if rather the worse for wear, boots on her bare feet.*
> *She greeted me politely, <u>her words conveyed with a lilt and flow not at all familiar to my ears</u>, and said that she and her husband Jubal Duvalier <u>had located</u> on <u>the third line to the west</u> of us.*
> *Her name was Hannah, she said, and she was looking for work, and, <u>as I had now</u> two babies to care for . . . .*

Reading the language of the period encourages us to suspend disbelief and accept the diary entry as "real."

2. The woman's vocabulary, sentence structure, and well-organized recollections suggest that she is literate and well-educated. She also seems relatively well off as she comments on Hannah's home-made clothes, rough-hewn boots, and bare feet. The woman is probably able to buy whatever she needs in the way of clothing. As well, since Hannah believes the woman may be able to afford to hire help, Hannah assumes she's reasonably affluent. There's also a suggestion that while the woman may not be used to seeing black people, she is not prejudiced in any way.

3. Actual phrasings will vary. One possibility is as follows: "*. . . would I be willing to hire her to help in the garden and around the house.*"

4. Answers will vary. This activity should be shared orally. Students will have much to learn from their peers' inventiveness and skill.

The Power of Simple Language

Big words and complicated sentence structure can often get in the way of effective writing. Plain language can also be deceptively simple. Sophisticated technique expressed in everyday language can produce the most vivid of impressions. In the powerful passage below from *Forbidden City*, William Bell purposely varies his sentence structure and powerfully uses simple language to craft an emotionally gripping and unforgettably dramatic scene.

In the story, Alex ultimately witnesses the tragedy of the 1989 massacre in Tiannanmen Square in Beijing, China. Heavily armed soldiers deliberately open fire on thousands of unarmed demonstrators, many of them university students. Alex's companion, Lao Xu, is killed. The thunder mentioned in this passage is the sound of gunfire.

> *Lao Xu spun around, his arms flung skyward. Before he fell the AK 47 spit flame again and the burst blew Lao Xu off his feet. His body slammed to the pavement, one leg caught under him, arms flung wide, his head twisted at an impossible angle. His blood began to run onto the road, a dark stream in the red light.*
>
> *Frozen, I stared at his still form. The thunder roared again. Someone beside me fell to the sidewalk. Someone fell against me, knocking me heavily to the ground on my back. Someone fell across my body, her head on my chest, facing me. There was a dark flower in the middle of her forehead. The flower slowly grew larger, then dark liquid trickled from it, flowing into her staring eye and across her cheek and onto my chest.*
>
> *I shrieked and struggled, pushing her slack body away as other bodies fell around me.*

1. The first paragraph explodes with horrific action, the flowing sentences capturing the movement with slow-motion precision. Compare the length and complexity of the sentences in paragraph two with those in paragraph one. How does the author change the type of sentences he uses? What effect does this change produce? Why does Bell "shift gears" at this point? When and why does he shift again?
2. Student writers are often warned about repetition in their writing. On the other hand, repetition wisely used can have a potent impact. What effect is produced by the repetition of *someone* and *fell* in the second paragraph? What effect is produced by using *body* at the beginning of this passage and then repeated near the end?
3. *There was a dark flower in the middle of her forehead. The flower slowly grew larger, then dark liquid trickled from it, flowing into her staring eye and across her cheek and onto my chest.*
   a. We often say that a metaphor is "apt," meaning that it suits the idea being described. Explain whether or not you think the flower metaphor is apt and why you feel that way.
   b. Writers are presented with choices in every sentence they create. Small details make a difference in how the reader responds. In this passage, why do you think Bell chose to use *eye* rather than *eyes*?
   c. In the second-last sentence, what effect is produced by the repetition of *and*?
   d. The comma after *larger* is an example of a comma splice. Bell deliberately included this obvious punctuation error. Imagine the sentence with a period used instead of the comma. How would that correction have changed the impact of the sentence and why did Bell prefer to use the comma splice?

The Power of Simple Language

Note: Before assigning this activity, please review the content of the excerpted passages from *Forbidden City* in the student activity sheet. They describe the massacre in Tiannanmen in specific, vivid, and powerful manner. You are the best judge as to how appropriate this material may be for your students.

Background

Grammar is a set of tools to enable communication, not a box of rules to contain it. Form follows function. By looking at how grammar can be shaped and molded to fit what needs to be said, students can bring a new focus and energy to their own writing. When students begin to imagine how grammar can be manipulated to enhance their messages, they begin to understand why they need to master the rules. The difference in perspective is crucial to emerging writers.

As students begin reading ever more sophisticated material, they become intrigued by adult vocabulary and complex sentence structure. Naturally, they try to cram as much of this "grown-up" language as possible into their own writing. As a result, their writing frequently becomes stilted, contorted, and impenetrable.

This activity offers a small window into the technical palette of a mature, knowledgeable writer. Students need to become aware of writing technique apart from "big" words and long sentences. They also need to get in touch with the power of plain, unadorned language used purposefully.

Learning objectives

- To examine the careful, purposeful techniques of a professional writer.
- To examine some basic grammatical rules and how they can be manipulated for effect.

Activity introduction

On June 4, 1989, in Beijing, China, thousands of citizens — many of them university students — gathered in Tiannanmen Square to protest against corruption and repression. Communist government troops surrounded them and opened fire. Countless unarmed demonstrators were killed or wounded. The introduction to the student activity sheet continues from that point.

Answer key

The detailed answers in this key are supplied only as a shorthand guide to the content. They shouldn't be viewed as a standard against which student answers are judged. Depending on their age and stage of reading fluency, students will express these ideas in their own language and according to their own background and experiences.

As well, trying to identify why an author constructs a passage in a particular way is tricky. Only the author knows for sure. Also, sometimes authors inadvertently include effects that enhance their writing. On the other hand, when we can articulate how we respond to a piece of writing, trace what produced that feeling in us, and realize that others respond in a similar fashion, we can safely assume the effect was purposefully created.

1. When Lao Xu is killed, Alex is *frozen* or paralyzed with shock. The short, declarative sentences mirror his mental state. He is momentarily stunned, unable to feel or think. He can only record each separate event as it happens. The image of Lao Xu's death in the first paragraph is sketched in specific, horrific detail, ending in the dark stream of blood on the road. The contrasting simplicity of the language and sentence structure in the first five sentences of the second paragraph punctuates the effect of the death on Alex and on the readers. Instead of moving on from the image, we are jolted over and over again by the sentence structure.

2. The horrid, explicitly drawn death in the first paragraph is contrasted and reinforced by the impersonal *someone* falling in the second paragraph. As these nameless people fall all around Alex like trees cut down in a forest, one horror piles on top of another. Since their deaths are noted in the same plain manner, we transfer the image of Lao Xu's death to their deaths and see it in our minds happening over and over.

   The use of *body* in the first paragraph makes it clear that Lao Xu is now lifeless. When Alex finally emerges from his shock, shrieking, at the end of the passage, he then recognizes what his senses at first couldn't accept: Death now surrounds him everywhere in the form of the lifeless bodies.

3. a. Some students may say that flowers are beautiful and that they shouldn't be used in this way. They may feel it's confusing and that they weren't sure at first what was meant. Others may recognize that the ironic use of the *dark flower* metaphor only increases the hideousness of the wound: The act of murder becomes a true crime against nature. The metaphor forces the reader to view the murder as an unnatural act.

   The differences in perception will stem from the maturity of the reader. If they are able to articulate how they feel and why they feel that way, their answers are valid regardless of how apt they view the metaphor.

   b. This detail may have a profound effect on some readers and strike other readers as nitpicking. We tend to think of eyes in pairs. We say that the eyes are the gateway to the soul. We look into someone's eyes to see if they're telling the truth. When we are forced to focus on only one, staring, lifeless eye, we find the image unsettling and unnerving. A single eye is riveting. Students may say that the image is "creepy" or "weird." Even that expression of their horror is recognition that Bell touched them deeply with one small detail.

   c. In spite of our disgust at the image of blood flowing into that single eye, the *and's* lead us inexorably step by terrible step along with Alex to follow that flow back onto Alex himself.

   d. Bell wants us to watch the image unfold just like a pan shot in a movie, unbroken and unedited. Any other punctuation would force us to lose the momentum of the flow and lessen the impact waiting at the end of the sentence. This "error" is a prime example of a writer using punctuation for effect rather than sacrificing an impression for the sake of a rule.

Investigating Your Own Reading

Any time you're interested and drawn into a short story or novel, you have an opportunity to learn more about the craft of writing. This activity provides you with a number of options for conducting that kind of investigation.

Here's how you start:

- Choose a short story or a chapter or section of a novel you've enjoyed and admired.
- Read over the questions below with that story or novel in mind. There are no wrong answers. The questions are meant only to guide your examination of the material you've chosen.
- Choose the two or three groups of guiding questions that you think might suit that material.
- Analyze the author's style using the guiding questions and describe some of the effective techniques that have helped make this writing memorable.
- Answer the final reflection questions.

Guiding questions

- What traditional grammatical rules or usage conventions did the author modify (such as, single-word sentences, sentences without subjects or verbs, comma splices, run-on sentences, slang or informal language)? For each example, explain the effect you think the author was trying to create with this use of language.
- How did the author match a character's vocabulary and manner of expression with the character's age, maturity, background, or education?
- How did the author manipulate the length, rhythm, or punctuation of sentences to emphasize a character's emotional state of mind?
- What startling/unusual/effective words, phrases, expressions, or images caught your attention? What was it about the writing that interested or involved you emotionally? What connections can you make between how the writing was constructed and how you responded?
- Choose a section that you found exciting, suspenseful, moving, or involving. Look at such aspects of the writing as length of sentences, word order in the sentences, subordination of ideas, word choices, images, or unusual constructions. How did the style of the writing help produce the effect that drew your attention as you read?

Reflection questions

- What aspects of the writer's style do you plan to use in your own writing? What kind of effects do you hope to achieve?

Investigating Your Own Reading

Background
One of the least used reading activities — and one of the most important — calls on students to analyze and reflect on an author's style. This activity encourages students to thoughtfully examine and carefully analyze how an author manipulates language for specific purposes. Students are then asked to reflect on what they've learned through their investigations and how they plan to apply what they've learned to their own writing.

The activity can be applied to any novel or story and is particularly effective with individualized reading materials.

Choice is crucial even when all students are examining the same reading selection. By self-selecting the cueing questions most applicable to their material and personal leanings, students can individualize the nature and direction of their investigations.

Impress on students that the cueing questions should be viewed as a starting point for their reflections. If they wish to elaborate on them, modify them, or add their own questions, they should feel free to do so.

Although there are no right or wrong answers to the questions in this activity, the exercise can be evaluated for the extent, depth, and quality of the answers. A sample evaluation rubric is supplied on the following page.

Learning objectives
• To practise analyzing how and why an author purposefully manipulates language.
• To reflect on how such stylistic features can be implemented in the students' own writing.

Activity introduction
The introduction to the student activity sheet will supply the necessary background for completing the assignment. Teachers need to decide beforehand the kind of reading material students will use to complete the activity and whether or not the evaluation rubric will be employed.

Answer key
If you plan to use the rubric, it is important to share it with students before they begin the activity so that they know how they will be evaluated.

Rubric for Investigating Your Own Reading

Student name: _____

Novel or story title: _____

Author: _____

When analyzing an author's style, how effectively did this student . . .

	Not Very	To Some Extent	Reasonably	Effectively	Very Effectively
• Complete all aspects of the assignment?	1	2	3	4	5
• Identify several effective stylistic techniques?	1	2	3	4	5
• Describe each stylistic technique as found in the story?	1	2	3	4	5
• Link *what* the author did with *why* it was done?	1	2	3	4	5
• Comment on own planned application of stylistic techniques?	1	2	3	4	5

Mark: ☐ /25

5 Creative grammar

It bears repeating — mainly because it's so hard to convince students — that the study of grammar is a means to an end and not an end in itself. As they complete exercise after exercise in a grammar text, study for another grammar test, or lose marks once again for faulty grammar in a composition, students understandably see getting "good" grades as their goal. The link between grammar and the language they use every day becomes tenuous. It doesn't help that some schools timetable a separate grammar period or even include a separate mark for grammar on their report cards.

For these reasons, the message that the study of grammar is a purposeful activity that has a direct impact on how effectively we express ourselves needs to be made manifest. Students need to see that the medium is the message. They also need to see how enjoyable and satisfying this medium can be.

The activities in this chapter establish a direct and intrinsic link between the "what" and the "why" of grammar. In each activity, one or more grammatical concepts are transformed into a creative outlet: The emphasis is on enabling expression. By the same token, in the process of writing within a specified structure, students come to a concrete apprehension of those underlying concepts: They learn by doing.

The activities range from the downright silly, such as inventing adverbial puns, to the clearly instructive, such as streamlining written descriptions. All invite students to individualize their responses and engage in grammatical challenges without fear of failure. There are no right or wrong answers in these activities, simply different ways of reaching the same goal. Some responses will be more effective than others, but all should be reasonably satisfying.

The sharing portion of these activities is vitally important. Students will be curious about how others have completed the challenges and will learn from what others have done. The teacher guidelines suggest ways to ensure that all students have the opportunity to present their results. In addition, most of the activities have a visual or graphic component: Bulletin board displays are a natural and important extension of the sharing process.

> The activities in this chapter invite students to individualize their responses and engage in grammatical challenges without fear of failure.

Grammatical Nuggets

A nugget is anything of value in a small quantity. If you restrict how much you can say about a subject and the format in which you say it, you can sometimes achieve added clarity and insight. Grammatical nuggets encourage that kind of expression in five lines.

> This song
> tender but deep
> echoes and resonates
> constantly
> in my mind.

Each nugget follows the same format:

Line 1: a determiner + noun (the topic or theme)

(*Note*: determiners are articles and words that take their place, such as *a, the, those, that, all, both*)

Line 2: an adjective (describing the noun) + a coordinate conjunction + another adjective (describing the noun)

(*Note*: coordinate conjunctions are words that join other words or phrases, such as *and, but, yet, or*)

Line 3: a verb (related to the noun) + a coordinate conjunction + another verb (related to the noun)

Line 4: an adverb (describing the verbs)

Line 5: a prepositional phrase (rounding off or finishing the thought)

Here's a list of some prepositions you might use:

about	above	across	after
against	along	amid	among
around	at	before	behind
below	beneath	beside	between
beyond	by	down	during
except	from	in	inside
into	like	near	off
on	onto	opposite	out
outside	over	past	round
since	through	throughout	to
toward	under	until	up
upon	with	within	without

Write three or four of your own grammatical nuggets. Choose one topic or theme and follow the format above. Select the nugget that most effectively illuminates your chosen theme. Be prepared to share this nugget in the manner your teacher suggests.

Grammatical Nuggets

Background   Some poetic forms, such as haiku, tanka, or diamante, purposely prescribe a limited and rigid format. The concise form often encourages clarity of thought and a revealing pointedness in expression. Brevity, after all, is the soul of wit.

Grammatical nuggets are restricted in format as well and for the same reason. A nugget is anything of value in a small quantity. This format's restricted nature often produces results that are rhythmic, trenchant, and poetic.

The format and the parts of speech that comprise the format are described in detail in the student activity sheet.

Learning objectives
- To review the following parts of speech: determiners, nouns, adjectives, conjunctions, verbs, adverbs, prepositional phrases.
- To explore self-expression in a concise and specified format.

Activity introduction   Place this nugget on the chalkboard and explain that it's expressed in a specified and limited form:

A cloud
white and wispy
swirling and drifting
slowly
out of sight.

Ask students to examine the nugget and comment on anything they notice about the construction that might explain how it's constructed.

Students might comment on the number of lines, the fragmented nature of the lines, or some of the parts of speech. When they've exhausted their observations, direct them to the student activity sheet.

Answer key   The simplest method of sharing results is to have students read aloud their favorite from the nuggets they've created. The results from this section can be shared orally in a combination of small and large groups. Sharing in small groups prior to sharing in the larger, class group has several advantages:

- sharing in a small group is less intimidating and embarrassing for students
- sharing in groups of four to six allows all students an opportunity to present their efforts to an audience
- students have a chance to gauge the effectiveness of their grammatical nuggets in the visible reactions of a smaller audience and to decide whether or not to risk exposing the material to the larger class group
- students have a chance to practise reading the material aloud prior to sharing in the larger class group

Here's one way the groups could operate:

a. The nuggets are read aloud in turn in the small group.
b. After the small groups are finished, ask for a volunteer from each group in turn to read aloud his or her favorite nugget to the larger class group. *No one* should volunteer someone else.
c. Continue moving through the groups on a volunteer basis for as long as time and interest allow.

Since the emphasis provided by the five-line structure adds to the appreciation, a bulletin board display of the nuggets should also be considered. Nuggets are easily set up on a word processor by aligning to the center. Students can also add colorful designs or appropriate drawings. You might want to give students the option of posting their nuggets anonymously.

"Tom Swifties" — Adverbial Puns

A popular series of old-time, adventure novels starred a boy named Tom Swift. Tom had almost superhuman abilities, but he also suffered from a language problem that many student writers also battle: Tom had a strange case of "adverbitis."

Whenever he said something, Tom could never just say it. He would say it *thoughtfully* or *breathlessly* or *brilliantly*. He overused adverbial modifiers so much that a special kind of joke, called a pun, made fun of the usage. A pun is a play on words and a "Tom Swifty" is a statement or question in which *what* is said is connected in a humorous way with *how* is it said.

> "I hope this eclipse is over soon," Tom said *darkly*.
> "Are you sure that milk is fresh?" Tom asked *sourly*.

Part A

In the five "Tom Swifties" below, the key adverbs have been omitted. Add the missing adverbs from the list below.

sourly	remotely	softly	sternly	downheartedly
ruefully	guardedly	gravely	fruitlessly	blankly
sweetly	sharply	dryly	brightly	testily

1. "Digging holes in cemetery is not my idea of a great part-time job," Tom said _____ .
2. "I'll turn on the TV without getting up," Tom said _____ .
3. "I don't want to go swimming," Tom said _____ .
4. "I think I just sat on a tack," Tom said _____ .
5. "I still have one more space to fill in on this application form," Tom said _____ .

Part B

Now that you have the idea, try making up your own "Tom Swifties."

1. Start with a list of adverbs ending in "ly," such as *playfully*, *hurriedly*, *brightly*, or *stormily*. You can use any of the unused adverbs from Part A. The larger your list, the easier it is to complete the next step.
2. Make a statement or ask a question that is linked to one of the adverbs, imaginatively of course. Try to create ten or even more if you can.

Part C

"Tom Swifties" also make excellent cartoons. Choose your favorite, illustrate it in cartoon form, and print the "Tom Swifty" below it as a caption.

"Tom Swifties" — Adverbial Puns

Background

If you want to send your students the message that grammar can be fun, this activity should do it. They get to enjoy silly jokes, make up their own, and draw some cartoons. At the same time, they learn about adverbs ending in "ly" and the connection between adverbs and verbs.

Learning objectives

- To learn to identify adverbs ending in "ly."
- To reinforce the relationship between adverbs and verbs.
- To create a positive attitude toward grammar instruction.

Activity introduction

Move directly to the student activity sheet. After reading the introduction, complete Part A orally. The answers are supplied in the answer key. Then assign Parts B and C.

Answer key

Part A

1. gravely   2. remotely   3. dryly   4. sharply   5. blankly

Part B

The results from this section can be shared orally in a combination of small and large groups. Sharing in small groups prior to sharing in the larger, class group has several advantages:

- sharing in a small group is less intimidating and embarrassing for students
- sharing in groups of four to six allows all students an opportunity to present their efforts to an audience
- students have a chance to gauge the effectiveness of their "Swifties" in the visible reactions of a smaller audience and to decide whether or not to risk exposing the material to the larger class group
- students have a chance to practise reading the material aloud prior to sharing in the larger class group

Here's one way the groups could operate:

a. The "Swifties" are read aloud in turn in the small group.
b. After the small groups are finished, ask for a volunteer from each group in turn to read aloud his or her favorite "Swifty" to the larger class group. *No one* should volunteer someone else.
c. Continue moving through the groups on a volunteer basis for as long as time and interest allow.

Part C

Posting the finished "Swifties" in a bulletin board display affords all students the opportunity to appreciate and enjoy the cartoons. The display also serves as a useful reinforcement when adverbs are next discussed.

Prepositional Poetry

A preposition is a word like *in*, *of*, or *among* that joins a noun (or a word that takes the place of a noun) to another word in the sentence. Notice that each line of the following poem begins with a preposition:

Where's The Wind?

Along the shore,
Above the sea,
Through the leaves,
Toward you and me;

Over the boardwalk,
Under the kite,
Beneath the sun,
Throughout the night!

Create your own prepositional poem:

1. Choose your own theme for a poem. It might be a pet, a feeling, a sport, an object, or anything at all.
2. Create your own phrases to describe your theme. Each phrase should start with a preposition. A list of some prepositions follows these instructions. Don't worry about the order; you get to rearrange the lines later if you wish. Remember that your poem doesn't have to rhyme.
3. Arrange the final phrases as a sheet of prepositional poetry. Move the order around until you find the arrangement that best suits your theme. Add an illustration.

Here's a list of some prepositions you might use:

aboard	about	above	across
after	against	along	amid
among	around	at	before
behind	below	beneath	beside
between	beyond	by	down
during	except	for	from
in	inside	into	like
near	of	off	on
onto	opposite	out	outside
over	past	round	since
through	throughout	to	toward
under	until	up	upon
with	within	without	

Prepositional Poetry

Background

Prepositions are confusing. Many students have trouble identifying them and figuring out what role they play in sentences. The wealth of different prepositions probably contributes to the confusion, but the main reason seems to be the action implied in a preposition. *Across* or *toward*, for example, seem so much like verbs that students confuse the two terms.

This activity tackles the confusion head-on. Rather than have them play "guess the preposition," students are given a large bank of prepositions and asked to make use of them. In the process, they become familiar with what a preposition looks like. By creating their own prepositional phrases, students come to an understanding about their appearance and purpose: They learn by doing.

Learning objectives

• To learn to identify prepositions and prepositional phrases.
• To practice self-expression through the creation of prepositional phrases.

Activity introduction

Introduce the activity with the poem "Where's The Wind?" on the student activity sheet. Read it aloud and explain that the poem is made up entirely of prepositional phrases: a preposition followed by nouns or pronouns. Explain further that each line of the poem has no subject or verb. Depending on the age and experience of the students, they may be able to deduce that the subject and verb for each line are implied in the title, i.e., subject — *the wind*; verb — *is*.

Answer key

1. Sharing poems in small groups prior to sharing in the larger, class group has several advantages:
   • sharing in a small group is less intimidating and embarrassing for students
   • sharing in groups of four to six allows all students an opportunity to present their efforts to an audience
   • students have a chance to gauge the effectiveness of their prepositional poems in the visible reactions of a smaller audience and to decide whether or not to risk exposing the material to the larger class group
   • students have a chance to practise reading the material aloud prior to sharing in the larger class group

   Here's one way the groups could operate:

   a. The poems are read aloud in turn in the small group and the illustrations displayed.
   b. *No discussion* about the relative merits of the poems is allowed. The audience can enjoy and learn from the poems without criticizing them.
   c. After the small groups are finished, ask for a volunteer from each group in turn to read aloud his or her poem to the larger class group. *No one* should volunteer someone else.
   d. *No discussion* about the relative merits of the poems is allowed. Instead, ask the students to identify from each description how a writing guideline was followed.

2. Posting the finished prepositional poems affords all students the opportunity to appreciate and enjoy the illustrations as well as all the poems. The display also serves as a useful reinforcement when prepositions are next discussed.

Writing Descriptions: Less Is More

The key to writing descriptions is not what you put in but what you leave out. You want to give your readers enough detail to ignite their imaginations but not so much that you stifle their interest. Choose your modifiers with care and your readers will do the rest.

Here are some guidelines when writing descriptions:

- In most cases, avoid being so literal and specific that visualization becomes difficult.

   Tom was 183 cm tall and weighed 54 kg.

   Put the same information in more general terms and let the readers fill in the rest from their own experiences.

   Tom was tall and slim.

- Avoid boring your readers by including too much unnecessary detail. Too much information operates like static on a television set, interfering with the picture you want to present.

   Rhonda wore light-blue jeans with a black belt, a yellow T-shirt with a red collar and red strips around the arms, a blue, long-peaked baseball cap, golden hoop earrings, and a small, gold chain around her neck.

   Instead, pick out a few distinctive details, present them, and save the rest for later. If you don't find an opportunity to include them later, they probably weren't important enough to include at all.

   Rhonda wore a yellow T-shirt tucked into jeans and a blue, long-peaked cap.

- Describe only those features or details that are prominent, distinctive, or are necessary to create a specific impression.

   A large, hawk-like nose perched proudly over his wide, toothy smile.
   The small mountain lake gleamed emerald green in the sun.
   The dark circles around her eyes and her tight, strained smile made me realize
      something was wrong.

- Whenever possible, base your description of a person on someone you actually know or have met or have seen. Think of that image as your main building block. You can then add or subtract details as you like, even taking features from several people and forming a "composite." You create a composite when you take one person's hair, another's voice, and another's walk, for instance, and put them together in one person. By starting with the features of actual people, you can visualize a concrete, specific image. Once you have a general idea of how this person might look, you can make up details and change the appearance as you wish. Attitude, personality, and behavior can be assembled in much the same way.

Your challenge is to create a fictional character out of a composite of people you know, have met, or have seen. Think of this character involved in some characteristic action or conversation. The description will be far more interesting if something is happening in the scene. You could say, "As Ralph shuffled into the classroom, he . . . ." or "Down at his locker, Ralph was . . . ." or "Ralph was sitting in a corner of the cafeteria when he began to . . . ." or any of a thousand different openings. Try to create living, breathing characters involved in scenes from their lives.

When you've finished your rough draft, review the guidelines for writing descriptions at the beginning of this activity and revise as necessary.

Writing Descriptions: Less Is More

Background

Student writers often find themselves in a quandary when writing descriptions. Their primary interest lies with plot: what's happening; what's going to happen; how it's all going to come out in the end. Description is a secondary concern.

Their strong visual images of people and places complicate how they write about them. These images may be stereotypical, derivative, and clichéd, but they come full-blown in the student's mind's eye. Transcribing them for someone else seems repetitive and unnecessary. Surely the reader understands who these characters are; those same images must also automatically pop up in their minds. Besides, how do you find a thousand words to take the place of one mental image?

This struggle with description may be a function of the egocentricity that young people enjoy, their inexperience with the craft of writing, or the gap in their reading and writing vocabularies. It may even have something to do with the influence of television. The same cast of characters each week act out a different plot; you know who they are before the opening credits; what you don't know is what's going to happen to them this time. Whatever the reason, student writers have a hard time transforming the movies in their heads into a few, well-chosen words on paper.

Teachers try to help but the cure for the "description blues" is often worse than the disease. When students are directed to use specific, concrete details, they take the advice too literally:

> The red-headed, green-eyed police officer with a big nose chased the blond, bushy-haired, blue-eyed criminal with crooked teeth down the alleyway.

When coached to give the reader enough detail to let them see exactly what the writer sees, they go overboard:

> Shambrae adjusted the red and gold baseball cap with the light blue trim on her gold-streaked, shoulder-length, jet-black hair that fell on the shoulders of her navy-blue, high-collared, red-buttoned, tight-waisted, full-length, suede coat.

While there's no instant panacea for the problematic issue of writing descriptions, this activity is a place to start. The exercise attempts to sort through student misconceptions and misapprehensions and offer some plain, direct, and easy-to-follow guidelines.

Learning objectives

- To learn some basic guidelines for writing descriptions.
- To practise writing descriptions following those guidelines.

Activity introduction

A good place to start might be with what students already know or think they know about writing descriptions.

Ask them what advice they'd give someone who wanted to know how to write effective descriptions of people or places. As they reply, fill in a chalkboard flow chart similar to the one on the following page:

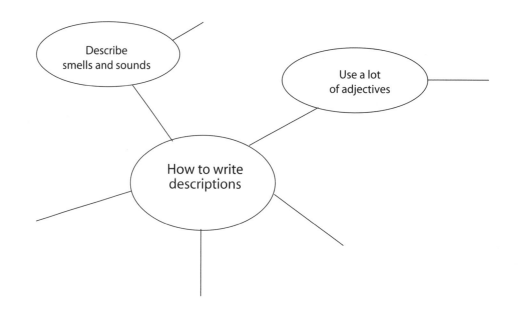

Sharing these descriptions in small groups prior to sharing in the larger, class group has several advantages:

- sharing in a small group is less intimidating and embarrassing for students
- sharing in groups of four to six allows all students an opportunity to present their efforts to an audience
- students have a chance to gauge the effectiveness of their descriptions in the visible reactions of a smaller audience and to decide whether or not to risk exposing the material to the larger class group
- students have a chance to practise reading the material aloud prior to sharing in the larger class group

Here's one way the groups could operate:

a. The descriptions are read aloud in turn in the small group.
b. *No discussion* about the relative merits of the descriptions is allowed. The audience can enjoy and learn from the presentations without criticizing them.
c. After the small groups are finished, ask for a volunteer from each group in turn to read aloud his or her description to the larger class group. *No one* should volunteer someone else.
d. *No discussion* about the relative merits of the descriptions is allowed. Instead, ask the students to identify from each description how a writing guideline was followed.

Accidental Narratives

Normally we decide what we want to say first and then choose the words that will best convey our meaning. In this activity, you'll be choosing your words first and discovering the meaning afterwards.

Complete each part in order as directed.

Part A

Write five sets of adjectives in the following order: number (more than one), size, color. For example, *three, small, red.*

1. _____ _____ _____
2. _____ _____ _____
3. _____ _____ _____
4. _____ _____ _____
5. _____ _____ _____

Part B

Write five plural nouns. For example, *horses.*

1. _____
2. _____
3. _____
4. _____
5. _____

Part C

Write five actions verbs in the past tense. For example, *floated.*

1. _____
2. _____
3. _____
4. _____
5. _____

Accidental Narratives — *continued*

Part D

Write five adverbs ending in "ly." For example, *lazily*.

1. _____
2. _____
3. _____
4. _____
5. _____

Part E

Write five prepositional phrases. For example, *around the corner*.

1. _____
2. _____
3. _____
4. _____
5. _____

Part F

Create five sentences writing your answers in the following order:

a. A1, B2, C3, D4, E5

b. A2, B3, C4, D5, E1

c. A3, B4, C5, D1, E2

d. A4, B5, C1, D2, E3

e. A5, B1, C2, D3, E4

Accidental Narratives

Background Although this activity has a serious intent, the end result should be fun. The students will first need to know the following terms and what they signify: adjectives, nouns, action verbs, adverbs ending in "ly," and prepositional phrases. The activity called Prepositional Poetry in this chapter is a useful introduction to prepositional phrases.

Learning objectives
- To review the following terms and what they signify: adjectives, nouns, action verbs, adverbs ending in "ly," and prepositional phrases.
- To create humorous sentences through spontaneous and unexpected juxtapositions.

Activity introduction You may want to use the following oral activity as an introduction to or as an extension of the written assignment.

Place the following list on the chalkboard:

1. an adjective of number, size, and color
2. a plural noun
3. an action verb in the past tense
4. an adverb ending in "ly"
5. a prepositional phrase

Divide the class into five groups. Assign each group to one of the items on the list. Each student in each group thinks of an answer for the number they've been assigned. Simply call on one student at random from each group, starting at number one, and enjoy the accidental narratives that unfold.

When you assign the written activity, reinforce that the sections should be completed in the order in which they appear.

Answer key Answers will vary. The sample phrases from the student activity sheet combine to produce the following sentence: *Three, small, red horses floated lazily around the corner.* Students can share their results orally. Be prepared for a zany session.

Dueling "Diamonds"

A diamante is a type of shape poem: the name derives from the Italian for diamond. A diamante poem is shaped like a diamond. This special kind of diamante is created around opposites or antonyms, almost like a duel. Here's an example:

Cat
soft, affectionate
purring, pouncing, meowing
catnip, mice, stick, fleas
racing, jumping, yelping
hyperactive, loud
Dog

A diamante poem has seven lines. The poem progresses from the subject at the top to a different and opposite subject at the bottom. The lines are structured in a specific way:

1. one noun, capitalized (This is the first subject of the poem.)
2. two adjectives (These describe the first subject.)
3. three participles (These end in "ing" and relate to the behavior of the first subject.)
4. four nouns (The first two have a connection with the first subject; the second two nouns have a connection with the second subject found at line seven.)
5. three participles (These end in "ing" and relate to the behavior of the second subject.)
6. two adjectives (These describe the second subject.)
7. one noun, capitalized (This is the second subject of the poem.)

To create your own diamante, follow these steps:

Step 1: Brainstorm a list of antonyms, such as *day/night, bully/friend, school/mall,* or *weekday/weekend,* and choose one pair.

Step 2. Place one of the antonyms at line 1 and the other at line 7.

Step 3. Following the structure given above, work from both ends toward the middle.

Your challenge is to create at least five diamantes. Choose the one or two you most prefer and prepare to share them as your teacher directs.

Dueling "Diamonds"

Background The student activity sheet is self-explanatory. The object of the exercise is to cast basic parts of speech in a different and creative light. Since the concept load is light, students will be able to confidently utilize grammatical terms in a simple form of self-expression. You might want to add the option of using synonyms instead of antonyms at lines 1 and 7.

Learning objectives
- To review nouns, verbs, participles, and antonyms.
- To explore self-expression through diamante poetry.

Activity introduction Place the following diamantes on the chalkboard:

School
challenging, boring
writing, reading, listening
tests, rules, friends fun
shopping, talking, eating
crowded, noisy
Mall

Weekday
busy, frantic
working, grinding, racing
school, homework, movies, friends
laughing, relaxing, hanging out
free, cool
Weekend

Explain that these are examples of a special kind of shape poem. Ask students to examine the poems and comment on anything they notice about the poems that might explain how they are constructed.

Students might comment on the number of words in each line, the use of antonyms, the divided nature of the poems, the shape, or some of the parts of speech. When they've exhausted their observations, direct them to the student activity sheet.

Answer key The students' diamantes can be shared in a number of ways. The simplest is to have students read aloud their favorite from the poems they've created. Since the diamond shape is intrinsic to this kind of poetry, however, a display of poems is a better option. Diamantes are easily set up on a word processor by aligning to the center. Students can also add colorful designs or appropriate drawings.

Suitcase Words

Lewis Carroll, the author of *Alice's Adventures in Wonderland* and *Through the Looking Glass*, invented expressions he called "portmanteau" or suitcase words. He took bits and pieces of two or three known words, packed them together, and created a totally new word or "suitcase" to carry the new, assembled meaning. These kinds of words are sometimes known as "blends."

When the hero of Carroll's poem "Jabberwocky" comes *galloping* back in *triumph*, he comes *galumphing* back. This word has actually become a part of the English language and is listed in some dictionaries.

While many portmanteau words drop quickly out of use, others become standard expressions.

Part A

Write the popular portmanteau words created from the following pairs:

1. motor + hotel = _____
2. horrible + tremendous = _____
3. splash + sputter = _____
4. flame + glare = _____
5. chuckle + snort = _____
6. breakfast + lunch = _____
7. sports + broadcast = _____
8. smoke + fog = _____
9. growl + rumble = _____
10. quasi + stellar = _____
11. quell + squelch = _____
12. squirm + wiggle = _____
13. simultaneous + broadcast = _____
14. television + evangelist = _____
15. aerobic + exercise = _____

Part B

Invent at least five portmanteau words of your own.

    class + boring = cloring
    permanent + pencil = permancil

Suitcase Words

Background: In Lewis Carroll's *Through the Looking Glass*, Alice recites the first verse of the poem "Jabberwocky."

> 'Twas brillig, and the slithy toves
> Did gyre and gimble in the wabe:
> All mimsy were the borogroves,
> And the mome raths outgrabe.

She then asks Humpty Dumpty to explain what the words mean since he had said "I can explain all the poems that were ever invented — and a good many that haven't been invented just yet."

In the process of his explanation, he mentions that *slithy* means *lithe* and *slimy* and continues "You see it's like a portmanteau — there are two meanings packed up into one word." A portmanteau was a case or trunk, usually made of leather, used for carrying personal belongings, such as clothes, on journeys. Humpty Dumpty further explains that *mimsy* is a combination of *flimsy* and *miserable*.

Since Carroll's time, many other blends have been proposed. Most pass by the wayside and are never heard again; others endure and become a useful part of the language.

Learning objectives
- To introduce students to the concept of blends.
- To familiarize them with popular blends.
- To give them the opportunity to create their own blends.

Activity introduction

If you have a copy of *Through The Looking Glass*, introduce this activity by reading the section that introduces portmanteau words (Chapter 6: Humpty Dumpty). Otherwise, place the equation "smoke + fog = ?" on the chalkboard and ask students for the word that means a combination of smoke and fog.

Explain that new words are constantly being introduced into the language as new technologies, discoveries, and concepts require them. Blends are one way to acquire these words.

Discuss the background to portmanteau words offered in both the teacher guideline and student activity sheet. Discuss and assign the student activity.

Answer key   *Part A*

1. motel	6. brunch	11. squelch
2. horrendous	7. sportscast	12. squiggle
3. splutter	8. smog	13. simulcast
4. flare	9. grumble	14. televangelist
5. chortle	10. quasar	15. aerobicise

Part B

Answers will vary as to the new portmanteau words. Share the results orally.

Cooperative "Fractured" Fairy Tales

A "fractured" fairy tale is a traditional story or theme that's been altered or updated for humorous purposes. This activity is cooperative since you'll be writing your own fractured fairy tales as part of a team.

Your fairy tales will be written in six steps. Everyone in your group takes a blank sheet of paper and completes step one. At that point, pass your paper to the person on your right and complete step two. Keep completing each step and passing your paper on until all six steps have been completed. Then return the papers to the people who began the story at step one.

Step One

Think of a fairy tale or a character who appears in a fairy tale. Don't worry about what's going to happen in the story. Someone else will take care of that for you. Instead, write a beginning or introductory sentence that starts "Once upon a time . . ." In this sentence, give the start of the story an unexpected twist. In the story your teacher read, the frog wanted to learn how to tap dance. You might invent a wicked witch who goes to charm school or a wolf who wants to play ice hockey. "Fracture" your fairy tale in any way you like.

When you finish your introductory sentence, **pass your story to the person on your right** and the person on your left will pass you their story.

Step Two

Read the introductory sentence on the paper you've received. Someone else will later continue the plot of the story. Your task is to write a second sentence including as many descriptive details as you can about anything that was mentioned in the first sentence. Feel free to add details that seem a bit unusual for the character. The frog who wanted to learn to tap dance, for example, was extremely clumsy.

When you finish your sentence, **pass the story to the person on your right** and the person on your left will pass you a story.

Step Three

The task at this stage is to write a sentence that introduces some problem to the story. Whatever the character or characters want to do, you're going to put some obstacle in their path. It doesn't have to be huge problem to be effective. The frog, for example, couldn't find a tap dance teacher.

Whatever the content of your sentence, you must include one subordinate clause. A subordinate clause begins with a subordinate conjunction. Subordinate conjunctions, such as *unless, when, while, since,* or *although,* are used when it makes more sense to show a cause and effect relationship or emphasize the order in which things happen. Subordinate conjunctions make one idea dependent on another. In the story, the statement that the frog had money for lessons is joined using the subordinate conjunction *although* to the statement that he couldn't find a teacher.

Cooperative "Fractured" Fairy Tales — *continued*

When you finish your sentence, **pass the story to the person on your right** and the person on your left will pass you a story.

Step Four

After reading through the story to this point, you're going to add a sentence that continues the action of the story. Your sentence must include one or more prepositional phrases. In the sample story, the frog searched "*in his pond, under all the rocks, and all through the forest.*" (The prepositional phrases have been highlighted.)

When you finish your sentence, **pass the story to the person on your right** and the person on your left will pass you a story.

Step Five

After reading the story you've received, add a sentence that resolves all of the problems in the plot. It doesn't matter how far-fetched or fanciful your solution is: one way or another, it's up to you to get things settled.

When you finish your sentence, **pass the story to the person on your right** and the person on your left will pass you a story.

Step Six

You have two tasks to perform. The first is to write a concluding sentence to the story that ends in a "tag" question. The sample story ended with the sentence, "He was a pretty smart frog, wasn't he?"

When you've written your concluding sentence, give the fairy tale a title and hand it back to the person who wrote the first sentence.

Your teacher will direct the next steps.

Cooperative "Fractured" Fairy Tales

Background   Students will have little difficulty with this activity if they've already completed A Game Of 'Tag' from Chapter 2, Sentence Combining Challenges: Conjunctions, from Chapter 4, and Prepositional Poetry from Chapter 5.

Learning objectives

- To review the use of modifiers, subordination, prepositional phrases, and "tag" questions.
- To write "fractured" fairy tales in a cooperative manner.

Activity introduction   Introduce the activity by reading aloud the following "fractured" fairy tale. The student activity sheet contains an explanation of the activity and a step-by-step blueprint for students to follow as they complete their own stories. The students should work in groups of four to six members.

The Frog Who Wanted to Tap Dance

Once upon a time, a frog named Harry wanted to learn how to tap dance. Harry was a small, green, near-sighted frog with two very large and very clumsy webbed feet. Although he had money for tap dance lessons, Harry couldn't find a dance teacher. He searched in his pond, under all the rocks, and all through the forest. Harry finally decided to pay for scuba diving lessons instead. He was a pretty smart frog, wasn't he?

Answer key

1. Have the students read aloud their own finished "fractured" fairy tales in turn in their small groups. The object is to enjoy the final product, not to critique the stories.
2. Ask for a volunteer from each group to read aloud a fairy tale to the whole class group. If time allows, return to the groups for a second or third volunteer.

6 Changing rules and suitable terms

Times change and so does language. A language exists in a context of people and time, and over time people modify how they communicate. At one time, for instance, upper-class speakers considered *ain't* the epitome of fashionable usage. Certainly we'll continue to keep *ain't* in its improper place, but we may have to shut our ears when we hear "I'm going to get a make-up test, aren't I?" Unless we're prepared to do battle every day for *am I not*, such compromises make eminent sense.

Beleaguered teachers are tugged on one side by the traditional usage they and the students' parents learned in school and on the other by contemporary usage in popular literature, print and electronic media, and spoken vernacular. What's the correct pronunciation for *behemoth* or *formidable*? Should you start a sentence with *because*? Should you ever accept the word *gotten*? In the shifting sands of evolving usage, where should teachers draw the line and when should they find some middle ground?

Language also reflects our values. Changing societal attitudes toward equity issues require teachers to instruct their students in the proper language to articulate those issues. While teachers usually feel confident adopting classroom-appropriate terminology for racial, ethnocultural, and religious matters, many still have to acquire and adopt suitable terms to further gender equity, for example, or to normalize discussions of sexual orientation. How far should teachers go in the search for gender-neutral language and what words should they use to discuss issues relatively new to classroom programs?

Except in dusty classroom language texts, language is in a constant state of flux. Usage once considered faulty may now either inhabit a gray area of stylistic choice or be fully accepted as correct and appropriate. The shifts in a society's attitudes, values, needs, and conventions are mirrored in modifications to grammar, pronunciation, and vocabulary. When the language has moved on, teachers need to pass this knowledge on to their students to help them make sense of and cope with their world. This chapter explores some of those modifications in contemporary usage and what they might mean for classroom programs.

> Language is in a constant state of flux. Usage once considered faulty may now either inhabit a gray area of stylistic choice or be fully accepted as correct and appropriate.

American English vs. British English

In the past, the 49th parallel acted as an invisible language barrier. North of the border, people observed the Queen's English; south of the border, they used a hybrid English all their own. The differences between the two were recognized and acknowledged and the respective conventions were taught in school. Over time, however, that great language divide has been shrinking and teachers have a number of decisions to make about the language they should accept from their students.

Should teachers insist that students use the word *fall* (American), for example, or *autumn* (British) or should they accept either or both? Should students talk about the building of a *railroad* (American) or a *railway* (British)? Most people probably don't discriminate between these kinds of synonyms. With vocabulary, we tend to accept whatever vocabulary is in the vernacular. The crux of the matter is getting our meaning across to others. If people understand what we mean whether we use *fall* or *autumn*, then either or both would be acceptable. Unless a story is set in England, however, few people in North America will understand that *boot* refers to a car's *trunk*.

Spelling is an entirely different matter. In speech, regardless of accent or dialect, *meter* and *metre* sound the same. When it comes time to write the words down, on the other hand, which spelling is correct and which is an error? If you live in the United States, you don't have a problem. If you live in Canada, you do.

With spelling, students are persuaded first by the word processing program they're using. If it's American-based and you're insisting on a British-only policy, be prepared for a struggle. If you're looking for reinforcement from the dictionary on this issue, you'll only find your stand compromised: American dictionaries are consistent with American English and Canadian- and British-based dictionaries accept both.

The problem is further compounded by the inescapable influence of American culture and technology. Whether students are downloading material from an American Web site, reading the rock lyrics on a popular American CD, buying the latest American best seller, watching "Wheel of Fortune" or "Jeopardy" on television, or flipping through their favorite American magazine, they'll be immersed in American conventions. Economic considerations also add to the American influence.

As a Canadian teacher, what do you do about *color* and *colour*, *judgment* and *judgement*, or *leveled* and *levelled*? Should you insist on *flavor*, on the one hand, and allow *jewellery* on the other? Where do you find the time to sort through this usage minefield?

Students aren't being perverse if they can't keep it all straight. Who can? The best policy is one of honesty and tolerance. Help students first to become aware of the differences; they deserve to know why they exist. Establish your policy, but be prepared to be flexible. The best you can hope for is consistency. The spelling convention they use at the beginning of a piece of writing, for example, is the one they should use throughout. If students use *center* consistently, for example, and no meaning is lost, it's not the end of the world. You might want to mention it, if using *centre* is your policy, but it's not worth penalizing the usage.

Establish your policy, but be prepared to be flexible.

And beginning a sentence

The coordinate conjunction *and* joins the meaning of two separate sentences. It also splices two principal clauses within one sentence. And no formal rule says otherwise. While students should be cautioned about overusing this technique, they will find occasions when it will prove both helpful and effective.

Appropriate terminology

We differentiate among and categorize groups of people in a number of ways. Since students need to learn how to appropriately address these groups, we have to help guide them through the maze of terminology. The goal is to name these groups in as respectful a manner as possible.

As with language in general, ethnocultural and social labeling is constantly evolving. Sometimes members of a particular group are themselves divided on how they prefer to be addressed. With other groups, several terms are considered acceptable.

Discussions about appropriate terminology should focus on positive, acceptable usage rather than a review of offensive language.

A frank and open discussion at the beginning of the year can establish guidelines for some of the terms requiring immediate attention. Teachers might prefer to wait for an ad hoc context to arise before discussing other terms. The core of these discussions should focus on positive, acceptable usage rather than a review of offensive language.

Terms for country of origin are relatively straightforward and seldom misused or misinterpreted: *Canadian, American, Peruvian,* or *Nigerian,* for example, are clear and unambiguous. *Asian,* not *oriental,* is the correct term for people from Asia. When the specific country of origin is known, such as Vietnam or China, students should use *Vietnamese* or *Chinese,* not *Asian.* In geography classes, students may need to differentiate between *Middle Eastern* countries, those countries in Southwest Asia, and *Near Eastern* countries formed from former Soviet republics.

Students are especially sensitive to the use of terms referring to skin color or tone. Any discussion in this regard should include their own experiences and preferences. *Black* remains the most commonly used term for people in North America of African origin, although *African American* is preferred by many. *Person of color* and related phrases, such as *women of color,* are more inclusive ways to refer to a broad range of non-European people.

A number of suitable terms identify the first people who inhabited a region. *Native people, First Nations, aboriginal* or *indigenous people,* or *Native Americans* are examples. If students know the names by which specific groups of native people are known, they should use them: *Algonquin, Haida,* and *Cherokee* are examples. Northern aboriginal people are *Inuit.* The old term, *Eskimo,* is offensive.

People with a physical impairment are *disabled* and their impairments are *disabilities.* Students will encounter the term, *handicapped,* as in *handicapped parking,* but should be alerted to the fact that the term can be offensive. Phrases, such as *differently abled* or *physically challenged,* are often considered unnecessary euphemisms with condescending overtones. *Blind* is a perfectly acceptable term for someone who cannot see and *deaf* correctly identifies someone who cannot hear. The phrase, *hearing impaired,* suggests a partial loss of hearing.

Given the relative youth of your students, a discussion of the denotations and connotations of words for people of advanced years should prove fruitful and illuminating. *Old, elderly, senior,* and *senior citizen* are all frequently heard terms. From a student's perspective, is the teacher standing in front of them *old*? Would they also call that teacher *elderly*? Although society is still struggling with its attitudes toward and labeling of people of "a certain age," *senior* and *senior citizen* seem to be the most popular choices.

Sexual orientation is another category by which people are identified and which requires appropriate language. A sea change has occurred in society's attitude toward and understanding of sexual orientation. The school has a vital role to play in helping students acquire the appropriate language to discuss the issue. Lacking appropriate language, students resort to the homophobic epithets and slurs that block their understanding and fuel discrimination.

Teachers have a responsibility first to provide students with the proper terms and second to normalize the use of those terms by naturally and spontaneously employing those terms in class. Intent is crucial in the use of these terms. Teachers need to correct students each and every time they're applied offensively, for example, in the phrase, "That's so gay!"

Even though the language around sexual orientation is still evolving, the suggested terminology below has passed the test of time and affords young people sufficient positive language for their needs.

The contemporary term *gay* is generally accepted as a term referring to both men and women. While *homosexual* remains a legitimate synonym for *gay*, the term is deemed offensive when used to refer to specific individuals. Since *gay* is also often used to refer to men alone and *lesbian* to women, a more inclusive phrase denoting both men and women is *gay and lesbian. Two-spirited* is a term preferred by members of the aboriginal community.

Same-sex is another useful term coined to establish a context in which only one gender is involved: *same-sex friends* would denote only those people of your own gender. The term has broadened to create another substitute for homosexual, as in *same-sex couple* or *same-sex marriage*.

Keep in mind that attitudes toward and acceptance of terminology will be affected by the nature of the community in which you live. Young people in urban gay communities, for example, have developed a set of terms that generally transplant these suggested terms. Over time, some of these terms may enter into mainstream use. For the time being, however, teachers should be selective and cautious about their terminology to avoid any misinterpretation among their students.

Keep in mind that attitudes toward and acceptance of terminology will be affected by the nature of the community in which you live.

Because beginning a sentence

A "rule" that has passed into common wisdom and been perpetuated by any number of teachers and parents alike is that a sentence can't start with the word *because*. No wonder students are confused when they encounter the construction in books, newspapers, and magazines.

Because of my headache, I wasn't able to think clearly.

This arbitrary "rule" was probably invented by harried teachers trying to eliminate sentence fragments beginning with *because* from student compositions. Unfortunately, it's taken on a life of its own. There's no valid reason for barring this entirely acceptable construction.

But beginning a sentence

When used at the beginning of a sentence, *but* serves to alert readers to an exception in meaning from the sentence before. No formal rule excludes using *but* in this position. Stylistically, using *but* is preferable to using *however* at the beginning of a sentence. A single, emphatic syllable, *but* gets the idea across faster and less obtrusively than *however*, allowing the reader to concentrate on the meaning that follows.

When used at the beginning of a sentence, *but* serves to alert readers to an exception in meaning from the sentence before.

Can and *may*

Student: Can I go to the washroom?
Teacher: I don't really know if you can or not, but you certainly may!

As students, we heard this groaner from our teachers and now we pass it along to our students. But brace yourselves; your students have some justification for this use of *can*.

If you explain the difference between *can* and *may* to students and then give them an exercise based on that distinction, they'll have no trouble with it. But the next time someone's thirsty, you'll hear *Can I get a drink of water?*

Why do students have so much difficulty with this usage in their daily lives? The problem isn't in their intellectual understanding: The concept is straightforward.

Can denotes an ability or capacity to do something.

> She can play basketball like a pro.
> He can do those math equations in his head.

May gives permission or suggests a possibility of something happening.

> You *may* get a drink.
> I *may* buy that jacket if it doesn't cost too much.

Part of the problem with maintaining this distinction is a gap in the language itself. We no longer use the tags *mayn't I* and *may I not* either in speech or in writing. Instead, we've filled the gap with forms of *can*.

> Can't I have the car Thursday night?
> Why can't she go to the movies this weekend?"

It's not much of a leap to go from *Can't I go to the washroom?* to *Can I go to the washroom?*

We also tend to use *can* as a more forceful way of denying permission.

> You can't borrow my homework. Do your own.
> No, you can't go out tonight. You're grounded.

This usage blurs the distinction between *can* and *may* even more.

Students should still be taught the traditional difference between *can* and *may*. But teachers should also realize that students are not being deliberately opaque or perverse when they use *can* for permission. Except in formal situations, it's the usage most people prefer.

Gotten

If there's no such word as *gotten*, why is it used so much? While many English teachers consider the usage controversial, a case can be made for *gotten*. Notice the difference in meaning in the following sentences:

> I have got to do homework for English.
> I have gotten to do homework for English.

In the first example, the individual has a current need or responsibility to do the homework. In the second example, the individual has had the opportunity in the past to do homework.

Another distinction comes out in these sentences:

> I haven't got any homework.
> I haven't gotten any homework.

In the first example, the individual has probably finished the work normally assigned for homework. In the second example, the teacher hasn't assigned any homework over a period of time.

That same sense of a process over time is often expressed in such sentences as this one:

> I've slowly gotten used to wearing braces.

People have discovered a useful way to say what they need to say by differentiating between *got* and *gotten*. While the usage may rankle purists, it seems to be here to stay.

He as a gender-neutral pronoun

Should *he*, *him*, and *his* be used as generic or gender-neutral singular pronouns? If not, why not? If not, how do you replace them?

In the past, many positions and occupations, such as politician, police officer, or doctor, were exclusively male. In those days, a sentence, such as "The doctor operated on his patient," would have been appropriate: All doctors were male. The masculine pronoun wasn't really gender neutral, but a reflection of the reality at that time. Now that times have changed, language needs to reflect that change.

Fortunately, there are a number of options that teachers can pass on to students for converting the so-called generic *he* to a truly gender-neutral usage. Some are more awkward than others and some are more suited to specific situations than others.

Now that times have changed, language needs to reflect that change regarding use of *he* as a gender-neutral pronoun.

1. Whenever possible, write in the plural. A sentence, such as *A student should always do his homework.* easily converts to *Students should always do their homework.*

2. Whenever possible, replace the pronoun with an indefinite or definite article or with nothing. *A successful teacher learns how to handle his paperwork.* converts either to *A successful teacher knows how to handle the paperwork.* or *A successful teacher knows how to handle paperwork.*

3. Repeat the noun instead of using a pronoun. *If a teacher hasn't got time to mark an exam, he shouldn't give it.* converts to *If a teacher hasn't got time to mark an exam, the teacher shouldn't give it.*

4. Use the relative pronoun *who* in sentences with *if*. In this case, *If a teacher hasn't got time to mark an exam, he shouldn't give it.* converts to *A teacher who hasn't got time to mark an exam shouldn't give it.*

5. Use such forms as *he or she* or *her/him*. This option is most useful in casual speech when the speaker gets halfway through a sentence and realizes a gender-neutral pronoun is required. While this solution is acceptable in writing when applied occasionally, frequent use can interfere with fluency.

6. Alternate *he* and *she* in successive sentences or paragraphs. This awkward practice should be reserved for situations in which the context requires repeated use of a generic pronoun.

Hopefully

Teachers have traditionally defined adverbs as words that modify verbs, adjectives, other adverbs, and clauses. Contemporary references add *sentences* to that list. In the following three examples, an adverb modifies a sentence.

> Hopefully, our plane will land safely.
> Thankfully, it did.
> Regrettably, we have to fly again.

Teachers who accept the last two examples often bridle at accepting the first, insisting instead that the adverb be replaced by *it is to be hoped*. They may be on shaky ground. This use of *hopefully* found common acceptance, and it's difficult to argue why it shouldn't. If you decide not to accept this use of the adverb, hopefully you'll be able to explain why.

Indefinite pronouns in a plural sense

The indefinite pronouns are *anyone, anybody, everyone, everybody, no one, nobody, someone,* and *somebody.* When acting as the subject of a sentence, they have traditionally been singular.

> Everybody is anxious at exam time.

Two contentious issues are slowly but surely changing this once invariable rule. The first is semantic. Sometimes the meaning of the sentence strongly suggests plurality.

Teachers have traditionally defined adverbs as words that modify verbs, adjectives, other adverbs, and clauses. Contemporary references add sentences *to that list.*

Everybody who studied for this test will get what they deserve.

The other issue is the trend toward accepting a singular sense for *they* in the search for gender-neutral pronouns.

Anyone who thinks they can pass this test without studying is misguided.

This trend is commonplace in everyday speech and increasingly acceptable in formal writing. Teachers should inform students of this movement and then let the language flow as it will.

Like

Young people have come up with several uses for the preposition *like* that English teachers never imagined.

Some time ago, *like* became a popular space filler between noun and verb phrases. The lingo of the day took on a madcap rhythm:

"Do you, like, know, like, the best places, to, like, snowboard?"

More enduringly, *like* is used instead of *about* to signal an approximation, often exaggerated for effect:

"The dog had to weigh like a tonne!"

Anyone associated with young people recognizes the latest, pervasive, and probably most enduring unconventional role *like* has assumed. *Like* has become a verbal signal that a quotation is about to be used:

"She was like I'm so bored and I was like Is that my problem?"

One of the problems with this newest use of *like* is that it has entered the vernacular so quickly and so pervasively. The majority of students find this usage convenient and effective. As the users age and as the trendy segment of the population picks it up, the usage is slowly creeping into the mainstream. Only time will tell if this adaptation of *like* is a fad or a grammar mutation.

For now, teachers have to find a middle ground. It's folly to deny young people their personal modes of expression, especially when everyone around them talks the way they do. To claim as teachers often do that "There's no such usage." flies in the face of reality.

On the other hand, teachers do need to make students aware of the conventional method for introducing a quotation in speech and indicate that this new usage should only be used in informal settings and among their peers. Otherwise, students run the risk of having what they say dismissed because of the way in which they say it. In formal situations, with people outside their peer group, and in writing, the usage must be modified.

It's folly to deny young people their personal modes of expression, especially when everyone around them talks the way they do.

Ms

The term *Ms* or *Ms.* has been around for over half a century. Both spellings are common. Since the term is not an abbreviation, as *Mr.* is for *Mister*, the period is unnecessary. *Ms* functions in exactly the same way when addressing women as *Mr.* does for addressing men. Whether a woman is married or single or has changed her name or not, *Ms* removes the need to guess or the chance of causing offence.

Ms functions in exactly the same way when addressing women as *Mr.* does for addressing men.

Ms is not a substitute for *Miss* alone. A list addressing married women as *Mrs.* and unmarried women as *Ms* defeats the term's purpose. If women express a clear preference for being addressed as *Mrs.* or *Miss*, of course, those terms should be used.

Prepositions ending a sentence

Never end a sentence with a preposition. Most references state that this "rule" probably stems from Latin. But it's a rule that can be dispensed with. In Latin grammar, prepositions never end sentences. English grammar, however, isn't Latin grammar.

Granted, whenever possible we should end a sentence with a word important to the meaning of the sentence. The reader is then left with a strong impression of the sentence. On the other hand, there's no need to tie language into stilted and unnatural knots trying to avoid a closing preposition. If it's a natural and functional way to express a thought, do it. When Winston Churchill was criticized for ending sentences with prepositions, he famously replied, "That is the type of errant pedantry up with which I shall not put." Case closed.

Pronunciation

When did people start pronouncing *formidable* with an emphasis on the second syllable? However long it's been, people seem to prefer this pronunciation to the traditional stress on the first syllable — even if reference texts are slow to accept it. As a teacher, how do you model correct usage if *integral* can be pronounced either with a stress on the first syllable or on the second? What do you do about *behemoth*, *harass*, *aberrant*, or *exquisite*?

Pronunciation shifts over time just like any other aspect of language. With television's all-encompassing influence, that shift can occur relatively quickly. An interview with a prominent British politician on a news program, for instance, could provide the catalyst for some people in North America pronouncing *despicable* with a stress on the first syllable; whether or not that usage catches on would be another matter.

We try year after year to get students to pronounce the first "c" in *arctic* only to discover that some references accept both pronunciations. Imagine the shock when we discover that both *arctic* and *Antarctic* were originally spelled in English without that troublesome "c."

With nautical terms, you can only shake your head. It's hard to explain to students steeped in phonics that *gunwale* rhymes with *tunnel* or that *boatswain* and *bosun* are pronounced the same way or that *leeward* can be pronounced as spelled or to rhyme with *steward*. There are only so many hours in a day.

As teachers, we can only model the language we've grown used to. At the same time, we have to keep an open mind about pronunciation. Who we are, where we live, and when we're living all influence how we communicate. The way we speak isn't written in stone.

Forget those dog-eared spellers as a reliable guide to contemporary pronunciation. We all need an up-to-date usage reference close at hand. As customary ways of speaking change, we need to understand and accept those changes for our students even if we choose not to adopt them for ourselves.

As customary ways of speaking change, we need to understand and accept those changes for our students even if we choose not to adopt them for ourselves.

Shall/will

A traditional explanation of the distinction between *shall* and *will* would probably read like this:

To show the simple future, use shall *in the first person and* will *in the second and third persons. To show the future of promise or determination, reverse this use.*

Over time, except for legal documents, this distinction between *shall* and *will* has virtually disappeared. *Shall* is still heard occasionally in questions requesting consent, such as "Shall we go to the movies in my car?" or "Shall we have the Sheldon's over for dinner?" But for the most part students have little context for reinforcing the traditional distinction. *Will* is perfectly acceptable in all cases.

So as a conjunction

It may be time to ease up on students using *so* as a conjunction. We used to teach that when *so* occurs in the middle of a sentence and can be paraphrased by *and so*, it is regarded as an error. That rule has become problematic.

Views about this construction have changed considerably since many teachers attended school. Many professional writers, for example, use the conjunction *so* by itself to stand for *so that* in clauses revealing the reason for an action. A sentence, such as "He did his homework on the bus so he wouldn't get a detention." is now deemed acceptable.

Either *so* or *so that* may also be used in clauses completing a cause and effect relationship.

I flunked two subjects so my parents grounded me for a month.

If you insist on a traditional approach to the conjunctive *so*, expect a frustrating time all round. Students not only have to recognize the error, they also have to identify the most effective way to correct it. Two of their options involve the semicolon, another problematic usage.

Using a period or semicolon to divide the two clauses, often produces short, choppy, unnatural-sounding sentences. Rephrasing with *and so* frequently sounds stilted or awkward and many students labor over the subordination of one clause to another. Perhaps students should be acquainted with the traditional rule and the options for correcting the so-called error and then informed that the rule is in the process of being revised.

Splitting infinitives

What's wrong with putting an adverb between the *to* and the verb in an infinitive? Some of the greatest writers in the English language have split their infinitives. Examples abound in popular books, magazines, and newspapers. Many times splitting the infinitive is the only way to avoid an awkward or ambiguous phrasing, as in the following examples.

> He was too angry to really listen to good advice.
> He was too angry really to listen to good advice.
> He was too angry to listen really to good advice.

This centuries old tradition again may be based on the fact that Latin contained one-word infinitives that couldn't be split; scant justification for insisting that students follow a rule that is broken daily in informal speech and formal writing.

If the meaning is clear and the rhythm reinforces the effectiveness of the phrasing, "To boldly go where no one has gone before" hardly needs tinkering with.

Some of the greatest writers in the English language have split their infinitives.

Final Words: Personalizing Grammar

Now that you've come to the end of *Grammarama*, it's safe to reveal a little secret about grammar instruction. The best grammar lessons don't always come from a grammar book, even this one; they come from the language you and your students use and encounter every day.

Grammar is everywhere: it's part of the fabric of our feelings, thoughts, and interactions. Newspapers, magazines, books, radio and television, song lyrics, the Internet, e-mail (*hw r u ? gr8! u 2?*), and the countless conversations that fill our days all form a vast reservoir of fascinating subject matter for use in the language classroom.

And when you find something worth sharing, accentuate the positive. While it's possible to uncover errors anywhere language is used, it's far more stimulating, instructive, and satisfying to find examples of language used well for students to appreciate and emulate.

Be on the lookout for phrases or images from your own life that grab your attention. Whenever a striking, vivid, apt, or unusual use of language attracts you, that kernel could form the core of an illuminating lesson for your students. Get into the habit of sharing with your students a stunning description from a novel you're reading, part of a persuasive essay from the newspaper, or a memorable line from a new song you've just heard. The more you put your personal stamp on your approach to grammar, the more your students benefit.

It bears repeating that grammar, like reading, is more caught than taught. As you model your own appreciation for well-crafted language, you reveal yourself as a lifelong language learner. You demonstrate to your students the kind of attentiveness to and appreciation of language you hope they will develop. You also enable their own search for personally significant language by talking them through your thought processes as you encountered whatever impressed, excited, or startled you about a particular language discovery.

The world of advertising is a particularly fruitful area to explore. Deconstructing advertising messages is not only a compelling pathway into exploring language practices, it's also an important life skill. Students are often unaware of how doggedly, cleverly, and insidiously they're pursued by advertisers. They can't turn on a radio or television, read a magazine, walk down a busy street, or ride a bus or subway without being bombarded by manipulative messages. Grammatical conventions are utilized, bent, and even broken in a calculated effort to entice, entertain, startle, persuade, pique curiosity, or even annoy. A slogan for a burger or a pair of running shoes can easily produce a unique teachable moment.

Your students can also teach you about their informal language and, in the process, personalize the study of grammar for themselves. They have a keen appreciation for the differences between the way adults use language and the way they and their peers do. Your students can inform you about the current slang or jargon in vogue. They can let you know about the catch phrases that are fresh and ubiquitous and those that have run their course. Enjoy their

As you model your own appreciation for well-crafted language, you reveal yourself as a lifelong language learner. You demonstrate to your students the kind of attentiveness to and appreciation of language you hope they will develop.

reactions when you disclose the slang and catch phrases popular when you were their age.

In all of your discussions about language, freely admit when you don't know the answer. The more students realize that you still struggle with usage the more you empower their own struggles. Offer to share in the research when an obscure or difficult point of grammar stumps everyone. Confess some of your own spelling and usage "demons" and share the tricks you use to manage them. Above all, resist placing adult standards on emerging language users. With age and experience, their fluency will grow.

Finally, when you model your own personal involvement with language and make room for your students to become personally involved, grammar is infused with relevance and immediacy. A grammar text becomes a jumping-off point, not a destination. Grammar can be as funny as a cartoon caption, as riveting as today's newspaper headline, or as transitory as the latest, TV-inspired catch phrase. Grammar is all around us to study and enjoy. Don't be afraid to open the classroom door and let it in.

When you model your own personal involvement with language and make room for your students to become personally involved, grammar is infused with relevance and immediacy.

Glossary

The definitions in this selected glossary reflect the meanings that are used in the text.

Active voice A verb whose subject is the performer of the action.
Adverbs Words that modify verbs, adjectives, other adverbs, or sentences.
Antonym A word meaning the opposite of another word.
Apostrophe (') This mark shows omissions, possession, or the plural of words that have no plural of their own.

Blend See **portmanteau**.
Brainstorming Generating a list of examples, ideas, or questions to illustrate, expand on, or explore a central idea or topic.

Closure The tendency to automatically fill in gaps in a message in a way that makes sense of the whole.
Cloze A written passage with selected words or portions of text strategically omitted.
Collaboration Problem solving in pairs and in other small groups (see also **cooperative learning**).
Colon (:) This punctuation mark is used to separate the main part of a sentence from an explanation, example, quotation, or list; also used after the salutation of a business letter, in certain numerical expressions, and between titles and subtitles in books.
Comma (,) The written equivalent of the pause in everyday speech that breaks a sentence or divides a word series to clarify and prevent ambiguity.
Comma splice Joining two independent statements into one using a comma alone.
Complex sentence A sentence comprised of one independent clause and one or more subordinate clauses.
Composition The process of putting words together to form an effective message or artistic statement.
Cooperative learning A variety of small-group instructional techniques focusing on peer collaboration.
Coordinate conjunctions Words, such as *or, and,* or *but* that connect words, phrases, or sentences that are equal in value and make sense joined together.
Correlative conjunctions Conjunctions used in pairs to connect two parts of a sentence, e.g., *either . . . or.*

Dangling participle A participle with no grammatical connection to the subject of the sentence.
Dash (—) The dash, represented by an unbroken line or by two hyphens, provides a break in a sentence for several reasons: to separate a parenthetical remark, to replace a colon, or to add emphasis in a series of statements separated by commas.
Declarative sentence A sentence that makes a statement.

Descriptive grammar An attempt to focus on the functional relationships within language that generate the basic principles; e.g., teaching the seven basic sentence patterns in English.

Determiners Words preceding a noun or pronoun limiting or particularizing the use of the noun, i.e., articles or words that displace them, such as *a, the, those, that, all, both;* sometimes referred to as noun markers.

Diamante A seven line poem shaped like a diamond.

Direct object A noun or noun substitute connected to the subject of a sentence through the action of a verb or that follows and relies on a preposition for its function in a sentence.

Ellipsis (...) A series of three dots used to indicate the omission of a word or words within or at the end of a sentence.

Evaluation Determining progress toward and attainment of specific goals; assessing student progress and achievement, and program effectiveness.

Fluency The ability to speak, write, or read aloud smoothly, easily, and with clear expression of ideas.

Grammar A study of the patterns of word formation in a language and the structure of word order in sentences, clauses, and phrases.

Haiku A type of Japanese poem written in seventeen syllables with three lines of five, seven, and five syllables, respectively, to express a single thought or evoke a specific response.

Hyphen (-) This mark is used to indicate that part of a word is carried over to the next line, to connect parts of a compound word, or in special circumstances with numbers.

Indirect object A noun or noun substitute that expresses to whom or for whom the action in a verb is meant.

Infinitive A verb that functions as a noun and is often preceded by *to.*

Literacy The ability to read and write; often extended today to include the processing of information from all sources and systems, including electronic and micro-electronic.

Literature Writing of high quality and significance because of a successful integration of such components as style, organization, language, and theme.

Metaphor A figure of speech in which a comparison of two different things is suggested but not explicitly stated.

Modifier A word or word group that limits or qualifies another word or word group.

Noun A word used to name a person, place, thing, quality, or event.

Paragraph One or more sentences about a single topic, grouped together, and usually with an indented first line.

Parallelism A stylistic technique in which equivalent syntactical structures are used in a series of clauses or phrases.

Participle A verb form used as an adjective or used with auxiliary verbs to form the passive voice and some tenses.

Parts of speech The traditional way of classifying words in English according to their form, use, or meaning in a sentence.

Passive voice A verb whose subject is the receiver of the action.

Period (.) The sign that signals the full pause at the end of a declarative sentence. A period can also highlight the use of an abbreviation.

Poem A composition, often in metrical form and rhyme, in which word images are selected and arranged to create an especially vivid, powerful, or beautiful impression on the listener or reader.

Portmanteau Invented expressions in which bits and pieces of two or three words are combined in one word; first introduced by Lewis Carroll. Also called blends.

Predeterminer A type of determiner or noun marker, called an *indefinite*, that can precede an article e.g., *all, both, half.*

Predicate The verb and associated words that inform about the subject of the sentence.

Preposition A word used to signal the relationship of a noun or noun substitute to another word in the sentence.

Prepositional phrase A preposition and its object.

Prescriptive grammar Teaching the rules that govern the use of language through such practices as sentence analysis, defining parts of speech, distinguishing between direct and indirect objects, transitive and intransitive verbs, or active and passive voice.

Principle clause An independent clause that can stand alone as a sentence but is used as only part of a sentence.

Pun A play on words having several meanings.

Punctuation The use of approved, specific marks other than letters to help clarify the meaning in something written.

Question mark (?) The punctuation mark used at the end of a sentence to indicate that the sentence is a sentence.

Quotation marks (" ") These marks are used to indicate the beginning and the end of a directly quoted passage or to enclose a word or phrase used in an unusual way.

Readalouds Any material read aloud, often by the teacher; can be fiction or nonfiction.

Run-on sentences Joining two independent statements into one without the appropriate punctuation.

Semantics The study of the meaning of words.

Semicolon (;) This punctuation mark is sometimes used to separate but still join two independent, but related statements; they also separate items in a series that already contain punctuation.

Sentence A word or words grouped together to convey meaning, often, but not always, containing two elements: what you are talking about (the subject) and what you want to say about it (the predicate).

Sentence analysis Identifying the parts of a sentence and the relationships that exist among them.

Sentence combining A teaching technique in which students build a single complex sentence from a series of simple sentences.

Simple sentence A single statement of fact in the form of a subject (what you are talking about) and a predicate (what you want to say about it).

Slang Expressions used in the informal speech or jargon of a particular group.

Subordinate clause A clause that can't stand alone as a sentence and is dependent for its meaning on the rest of the sentence.

Subject The word or word group that declares what the sentence is telling about.

Subordinate conjunctions Words, such *as unless, when, while, since,* or *although* that are used when it makes more sense to show a cause and effect relationship or emphasize the order in which things happen. Subordinate conjunctions make one idea dependent on another.

Syntax The pattern or structure of word order in sentences.

Tag A phrase added to the end of a sentence that changes a statement into a question.

Tanka An unrhymed adaptation of a Japanese poetic form consisting of five lines of five, seven, five, seven, and seven syllables respectively. A common English adaptation consists of five lines of 31 syllables or less divided among the lines as needed.

Transformational grammar Manipulating sentences in order to understand and increase fluency; includes expanding, rearranging and combining sentences.

Usage The customary or preferred way of using specific items of language in such areas as pronunciation, vocabulary, and syntax.

Verb A word or word grouping that expresses action, a state of being, a happening, or a command.

Verb, intransitive A verb that does not connect the subject to a direct object; some verbs can be intransitive and transitive. For example, in the sentence, *She played well,* the verb *played* does not connect the subject to an object and is therefore intransitive. In the sentence, *She played the guitar,* the same verb connects the subject to the object *guitar.*

Verb, transitive A verb that connects the subject to a direct object; some verbs can be transitive and intransitive. For example, in the sentence, *He reads science fiction novels,* the verb *reads* connects the subject to the object *science fiction novels* and is therefore transitive. In the sentence, *He reads every night,* the same verb does not connect the subject to an object and is intransitive.

Vernacular The contemporary spoken language of a community or the unique way words are used by a particular class or profession.

Word As author Frank Smith put it, a sequence of letters with white space on either side. These small units may contain meaning by themselves or help express meaning in association with other words.

Word order The sequence of words that determines meaning in a sentence.

Selected Bibliography

Berube, Margery S. *The American Heritage Book Of English Usage.* Boston: Houghton Mifflin Co., 1996.

Fitton, Caroline and Don McBeath. *Sentence Combining: Choices In Writing.* Scarborough, ON: Prentice-Hall Canada Inc., 1987.

Garner, Bryan A. *The Oxford Dictionary Of American Usage And Style.* New York: Oxford University Press, 2000.

Haussamen, Brock et al. *Grammar Alive! A Guide for Teachers.* Urbana, Illinois: National Council of Teachers of English, 2003.

O'Connor, Patricia T. *Woe Is I.* New York: Riverhead Books, 1996.

Parsons, Les. *Response Journals Revisited.* Markham, ON: Pembroke Publishers Ltd., 2001.

Quirk, Randolph, Sidney Greenbaum, Geoffrey Leech, and Jan Svartvik. *A Comprehensive Grammar of the English Language.* Essex, England: Longman, 1985.

Shuster, Edgar H. *Breaking The Rules: Liberating Writers Through Innovative Grammar Instruction.* Portsmouth, NH: Heinemann, 2003.

Strong, William. *Sentence Combining: A Composing Book.* 3rd ed. New York: McGraw-Hill, 1994.

Thompson, Geoff. *Introducing Functional Grammar.* London: Arnold, 1996.

Weaver, Constance. *Teaching Grammar in Context.* Portsmouth, NH: Boynton/Cook, 1996.

Index

Absolutely Invincible, 52, 56, 58
Accidental narratives, 83–85
Adjectives, 9, 10, 16, 17, 18, 29, 31, 39, 40, 72, 73, 83, 85, 86, 99
   General, 10, 18, 19
   Hyphenated phrasal, 54, 55
   Scrambled, 11, 17–19, 22
Adverbs, 39, 40, 72, 73, 75, 76, 84, 85, 99, 103
Alice's Adventures in Wonderland, 88
Although . . . nevertheless, 28, 29–30
Although . . . yet, 28, 30
American English vs. British English, 93–94
Analyzing sentences, 8
And beginning a sentence, 94
Antonyms, 86, 87
Appropriate terminology, 95–96
Articles, 10, 18, 72, 99
   Definite, 8, 99
   Indefinite, 99
Articulate, 61

Balancing nouns, 28
Balancing verb phrases, 28
Because beginning a sentence, 96
Bell, William, 52, 53, 54, 58, 61, 62, 65
Blends, 89
Both . . . and, 28, 29
But beginning a sentence, 97

Can and may, 97–98
Carroll, Lewis, 6, 8, 15, 88, 89
Clarifying the rules, 53–55
Cloze passages, 16
Combining sentences, 9, 34–51
Comma splices, 24–27, 65, 68
   Correcting, 24–25, 26
   Identifying, 24, 26
Commas, 24–27, 53, 54, 55, 65
Communication, 7
Complex questions
   Sentence-combining challenge, 46–47
Complex sentence structure, 10
Complex sentences, 10, 34, 37, 47, 50, 51
Composite, 79, 80
Concepts, 10
   Abstract, 43
Conjunctions, 48, 49
   Coordinate, 24, 26, 41, 43, 72, 94

Correlative, 28–30
   Sentence-combining challenge, 41–43
   So, 102
   Subordinate, 26, 41, 43, 90
Cooperative "fractured" fairy tales, 90–92
Coordinate conjunctions, 24, 26, 41, 43, 72, 94
Correcting the comma splice, 24–25, 26
Correlative conjunctions, 28–30
Creating a character's language, 61–64
Creative grammar, 11, 12, 71–92

Dangling participles, 31, 32
Dash, 53, 54, 55
Declarative sentences, 56, 67
Defining parts of speech, 8
Definite article, 8, 99
Descriptive grammar, 8, 9
Determiners, 10, 18, 72, 73
Diamante, 73, 86
Direct instruction, 10
Direct objects, 8
Disjointed sentences, 31–33, 37
Dueling "diamonds," 86–87

Either . . . or, 28
Ellipsis, 62
English as a second language, 7, 10, 13, 14, 18

Faulty parallel structures, 29
Forbidden City, 52, 53, 54, 65, 66
"Fractured" fairy tales, 90–92
Fundamentals, 37

A game of "tag," 13, 14
Gotten, 98
Grammar
   Creative, 11, 12, 71–92
   Definition, 8, 66
   Descriptive, 8, 9
   Personalizing, 104–105
   Prescriptive, 6, 7, 8
   Rules of, 52, 68
   Studying, 7, 8, 71, 104
   Teaching, 6, 7, 8
   Transformational, 8, 9–10
Grammar instruction, 7, 10, 11
Grammatical closure, 16
Grammatical nuggets, 72–74

Grammatically correct, 34, 37
Grammatically effective, 34
Guiding questions, 68

Haiku, 73
He as a gender-neutral pronoun, 98–99
Hopefully, 99
Humpty Dumpty, 6, 7, 89

Identifying the comma splice, 24, 26
If . . . then, 28, 30
Indefinite articles, 99
Indefinite pronouns in a plural sense, 99–100
Indirect objects, 8
Intelligence, 61
Interrogative pronouns, 43
Intransitive verbs, 8
Investigating your own reading, 68–69
   Rubric, 70

"Jabberwocky," 15, 88, 89
Joyce, James, 8
Just as . . . so, 28, 30

Like, 100
Literacy, 61

Manipulating sentence structure, 56–60
Matching parts: correlative conjunctions, 28–30
Matching prepositional phrases, 28
Metaphors, 65, 67
Modifiers, 9, 11, 26, 45, 48, 49, 79, 92
   Adverbial, 75
   Sentence-combining challenge, 39–40
Modifying phrases, 31
Ms, 101

Neither . . . nor, 28, 29
No Signature, 52, 61
Not only . . . but also, 28, 30
Noun phrases, 9
Nouns, 16, 17, 18, 26, 29, 55, 72, 73, 78, 83, 85, 86, 87, 99
   Balancing, 28
Numerals, 18

Object, 9
Objects
   Direct, 8
   Indirect, 8

Paragraph
    Definition, 58
Parallel constructions, 48, 49
    Sentence-combining challenge,
      44–45
Parallelism, 29
    Faulty, 29
Participle phrases, 31
Participles, 31, 32, 86, 87
    Dangling, 31, 32
Parts of speech, 16, 29, 73
    Defining, 8
Periods, 24, 26, 102
Personalizing grammar, 104–105
Phrasal adjectives, 54, 55
Phrases
    Modifying, 31
    Noun, 9
    Participle, 31
    Prepositional, 28, 72, 73, 78, 84, 85,
      91, 92
    Verb, 9, 28
Plain language, 65
Portmanteau words, 88, 89
Power of simple language, The, 65–67
Predeterminers, 10, 18, 19
Predicate, 34, 54, 56, 58, 59, 60
Prepositional phrases, 28, 72, 73, 78, 84,
    85, 91, 92
Prepositional poetry, 77–78
Prepositions, 16, 45, 72, 77, 78
Prepositions ending a sentence, 101
Prescriptive grammar, 6, 7, 8
Pronouns, 16, 78, 99
    He as gender-neutral, 98–99, 100
    Indefinite, 99–100
    Interrogative, 43
    Relative, 43, 99
Pronunciation, 8, 93, 101–102
Punctuation, 20, 22, 26, 59, 62, 65, 67,
    68

Readaloud, 8
Reading between the words, 15, 16
Reflection questions, 68
Relative pronouns, 43, 99
Routines, 37
Rubric for investigating your own
    reading, 70
Rules of grammar, 52, 68
Rules of writing, 53
Run-on sentences, 68

Scrambled adjectives, 11, 17–19, 22
Semicolons, 24, 26, 102
Sentence combining, 9, 34–51
Sentence-combining challenge
    Complex questions, 46–47
    Conjunctions, 41–43

Invent your own, 50–51
Modifiers, 39–40
Parallel constructions, 44–45
Test yourself, 48–49
Warm-ups, 36–38
Sentence fragments, 16, 56, 59
Sentence patterns, 9
Sentences
    Analyzing, 8
    Combining, 9, 34–51
    Complex, 10, 34, 37, 47, 50, 51
    Declarative, 56, 67
    Definition, 54, 58
    Dependent, 26
    Disjointed, 31–33, 37
    Ellipted, 9
    Expanding, 8
    Independent, 24, 26
    Meaning, 20
    Rearranging, 9, 22
    Rephrasing, 32
    Run-on, 68
    Simple, 34, 36, 37, 50, 51
Shall/will, 102
Simple questions, 46, 47
Simple sentences, 34, 36, 37, 50, 51
Since . . . therefore, 28, 30
Slang, 68, 104–105
So as a conjunction, 102
Spelling, 8, 52, 94
Splitting infinitives, 103
Stones, 52, 61
Studying grammar, 7, 8, 71, 104
Subject, 34, 54, 56, 58, 59, 60, 68, 78, 86
Subordinate clauses, 26, 27, 47, 90
Subordinate conjunctions, 26, 41, 43,
    90
Suitcase words, 88–89
Synonyms, 87, 94
Syntax, 8, 16

Tagging, 13, 14, 91, 92
Tanku, 73
Teacher guidelines
    Accidental narratives, 85
    Clarifying the rules, 54–55
    Cooperative "fractured" fairy tales,
      92
    Creating a character's language,
      63–64
    Dueling "diamonds," 87
    A game of "tag," 14
    Grammatical nuggets, 73–74
    Investigating your own reading, 69
    Manipulating sentence structure,
      58–60
    Matching parts: correlative
      conjunctions, 29–30
    Power simple language, The, 66–67

Prepositional poetry, 78
Reading between the words, 16
Scrambled adjectives, 18–19
Sentence-combining challenge:
    complex questions, 47
Sentence-combining challenge:
    conjunctions, 43
Sentence-combining challenge:
    invent your own, 51
Sentence-combining challenge:
    modifiers, 40
Sentence-combining challenge:
    parallel constructions, 45
Sentence-combining challenge: test
    yourself, 49
Sentence-combining challenge:
    warm-ups, 37–38
Suitcase words, 89
"Tom Swifties" — adverbial puns, 76
Unsplicing commas, 26–27
Word order combinations, 22–23
Writing descriptions: less is more,
    81–82
Teaching grammar, 6, 7, 8
Through the Looking Glass, 6, 15, 88, 89
"Tom Swifties" — adverbial puns,
    75–76
Transformational grammar, 8, 9–10
Transitive verbs, 8

Unsplicing commas, 24–27
Usage, 7, 8, 10, 14, 26, 52, 68, 93, 98,
    100
    Acceptable, 95
    Contemporary, 7
    Current, 7
    Gender-neutral, 98
    Informal, 9

Verb phrases, 9
    Balancing, 28
Verbs, 16, 24, 25, 26, 27, 31, 45, 53, 54,
    68, 72, 73, 76, 78, 83, 85, 87, 99, 103
    Intransitive, 8
    Transitive, 8
Vocabulary, 8, 63, 64, 66, 68, 93, 94
Voice
    Active, 8
    Passive, 8

When . . . then, 28, 30
Whether . . . or, 28, 30
Word order, 7, 10, 16, 17, 18, 20, 22, 62,
    68
Word order combinations, 20–23
Writing descriptions: less is more,
    79–82